*Also by Harry B. Ellis:*

HERITAGE OF THE DESERT
The Arabs and The Middle East
[*1956*]

ISRAEL AND THE MIDDLE EAST
[*1957*]

# CHALLENGE
## in the
# MIDDLE EAST

## Communist Influence and
## American Policy

HARRY B. ELLIS

THE RONALD PRESS COMPANY · NEW YORK

2

Library of Congress Catalog Card Number: 60–15030

To
Reggie

# Preface

From 1952 until the present I have worked with the problems of the Middle East, for more than half of that time as resident Middle East correspondent of *The Christian Science Monitor*. My work has taken me widely and repeatedly throughout the Arab world, and also to Israel, Turkey, and Iran.

In this book I have set down certain conclusions of my own about effective American policies in the area. The central problem I consider to be the safeguarding of legitimate American interests against the steady pressure of Communist infiltration. In the following pages I explain my reasons for believing that Arab leaders—notably President Nasser—are far more deeply concerned about the dangers of Communist influence than is realized by many in the West.

I also attempt to show that the national interests of the United States and those of the Arabs, Israelis, and other Middle Eastern peoples are compatible, whereas the national interests of the Soviet bloc and the nations of the

Middle East are not. This provides a framework within which a mutually satisfactory, though perhaps never ideal, relationship may be worked out between the United States and the Middle East.

In earlier books I have sought to recount, without overly intruding my own opinions, the histories of the Arabs and Jews and where these histories have led the two peoples, up to and including their present impasse over Palestine. This present book, by contrast, is far more personal in judgment. Its conclusions are based in part on background information, some of it never before published, about past American relations with Arab leaders, principally President Nasser. My conclusions also have been reached through conversations with prominent Middle Easterners at many levels, discussions with American and other diplomats, and firsthand acquaintance with the attitudes of "little" Arabs of the cities and farms.

Despite this personal quality it is my earnest hope that the book will be accepted as fair-minded by all parties involved in the complex conflicts of interest in the contemporary Middle East. Certainly its one conscious bias is that of an American observer looking at the area primarily from the standpoint of the interests of the United States.

HARRY B. ELLIS

Beirut, Lebanon
    August, 1960

# Contents

|  |  | PAGE |
|---|---|---|
| 1 | DYNAMITE AND AN EMPTY NET | 3 |
| 2 | "WHEN COMMUNISM ENTERS A COUNTRY" | 12 |
| 3 | CAIRO THROUGH WASHINGTON'S EYES | 31 |
| 4 | THE LONG ROAD BACK | 55 |
| 5 | THE UNITED STATES AND ISRAEL | 87 |
| 6 | AMERICAN INTERESTS IN THE MIDDLE EAST | 121 |
| 7 | WHERE DO THE SOVIETS STAND? | 143 |
| 8 | CHALLENGE TO YANKEE TRADERS | 180 |
| 9 | FOR TODAY AND TOMORROW | 202 |
|  | SELECTED BIBLIOGRAPHY | 227 |
|  | INDEX | 231 |

# CHALLENGE
## in the
# MIDDLE EAST

# CHAPTER 1

# Dynamite and an Empty Net

During a season of drought, as occurred in the spring of 1960, the countryside from Teheran south to Isfahan is dry as dust. At times the surface of the land is flat, at other times broken by high dunes made of hardpan and scree. Everywhere the landscape is the color of dust, even to the dried-mud villages through which the bumpy road passes.

So the countryside remains, a wilderness of emptiness, until, about seventy miles south of Teheran, the town of Qum lifts itself from the sands. A town of crumbling mud walls and abject poverty, yet one of the most breath-taking sights in all Iran, for soaring like a glory above the mud walls rises the great golden dome of Qum's sacred mosque.

Incredibly lovely, the dome floats above the town like a brilliant golden sun, while in the dirty crooked lanes below, dark-robed women squat by the open canals to

3

wash their laundry, and black-bearded men, many with hair close-cropped on their round heads, tend shop or urge on their donkeys through the streets.

What does their golden dome mean to the people of Qum? Enough, at any rate, that I, as a non-Moslem, was advised not to stop in the town during the religious holidays then in progress. So I did not, though I drank in the scene with my eyes until the golden dome had faded in the distance and the swirling dust of the desert road once more was all around.

There is another marvel to be seen on this road which passes through Qum on its way to southern Iran. Every few miles the traveler passes villages built of mud, and outside most of these villages is a curious sight. Mounds of earth, about forty feet apart, run in a straight line from the village toward some high hill or mountain in the distance, for all the world like a row of giant ant hills.

One line of mounds per village, like some fantastic chain of sand binding the town to the nearest hill. In fact it is just that, a chain without which the village could not live, for these mounds of earth are the visible signs of an underground canal carrying water from a mountain's height down to the village.

Of all the wonders of Iran, none seems to me more awe-inspiring than this ancient system of providing water for the arid villages of the country. Down through the centuries the men of Persia have tunneled, like human moles, straight down into the earth, and there—by some kind of mental mathematics worked out in total darkness—have dug by hand canals whose grade and pitch are calculated to keep water flowing at the desired rate from the mountain's spring to the village well.

The canals thus dug, dotting the countryside of Iran,

are called qhanats. They empty into a town both in wells and in open ditches running along the streets. In a single canal at any one time may be seen women dipping water for their household needs, other women washing pots and pans, little boys relieving themselves, and animals drinking.

This system of qhanat, and the labor it involves, may not seem impressive until one has seen it work in practice. A few miles south of Qum a row of earth mounds crossed the road and at one mound stood a man operating some kind of wooden frame. We stopped and went over to the man. As we watched, he began to revolve a hollow wooden drum supported by the frame, and a rope snaked up from a hole in the ground beneath. At the end of the rope came up a small leather bucket, filled with earth. This bucket the man emptied onto a growing mound of earth around the rim of the hole and lowered the bucket to the bottom.

Seventy yards down, that hole went, the man told my driver. Less than a yard in diameter, the sides of the hole were marked by dirt "steps," down which the digger let himself into the depths below. The man at the winch took out a pocket mirror and reflected the sun's rays toward the bottom of the hole. Far, far down something moved and a faint shout came up to the surface. That "something" was a qhanat digger, two hundred feet below the desert floor on which we stood.

Dozens of similar holes had been dug forty feet apart. But the real job was to dig a tunnel from the mountain to the village, and to grade the tunnel so that water would flow to the village site. Multiply the labor of that qhanat by many, many thousands and one has the general picture of much of Iran's water supply—a conception as wonderful today, in its tribute to human genius and courage and labor, as when it was invented thousands of years ago.

But what of the men who dig these amazing canals? What was "my" digger thinking, I wondered, as I peered down into his dark pit. His world was pitch dark; mine was flooded by warm spring sunshine. Had he climbed up and seen me, I would have been one of the people he saw occasionally flashing by in expensive cars, as strange to him as he was to me. That night he would sleep on the floor of a mud-walled room with the rest of his family. I would sleep in a hotel room which cost more each night than he earned in a week down there in the Stygian night of his canal. We lived in separate worlds.

So it is throughout the Middle East between Westerners and the local people among whom they move. Few Westerners pretend to understand the "little man" of the Middle East. What does the Kurdish porter of Aleppo think, bent so low beneath the refrigerator on his back that he can barely lift his head to see the cars churning about him on the street?

Or the peasant farmer, the fellah. How does one know his thoughts as he rolls clods of cattle dung flat on his roof to dry, later to be burned by his wife on their outdoor oven of mud? Nor can the foreigner fathom the thinking of the toilers of the suqs, or covered markets in Arab towns, who, in sunless shops, bend close over their hands, working brass, copper, and silver into trays which the camera-laden tourist will heft, finger, and perhaps buy.

I have seen construction workers at a great apartment house in Beirut drop their tools and crowd around to kiss the hand of a frail elderly Syrian, dressed in dark-blue Western suit and red fez, who stopped in his chauffeured car to inspect this building which he owned. What judgments, if any, did his workers cast on this man who, until land reform in Syria, had owned villages and vast tracts of wheat land, and who now invested his money in buildings in Beirut?

Many poor Arabs of the Middle East have not even the sanctuary or security of a home which truly belongs to them. A case in point are the people who live along a sandy stretch of beach south of Beirut. Before the Lebanese rebellion of 1958 this beach was empty of habitation. During that Moslem-led revolt which tore the country apart, certain Moslem leaders of Beirut, with an eye to their popular following, encouraged their supporters to settle along this attractive beach.

In their hundreds the settlers flocked in. Squatters is a better word, for the land belonged neither to them nor to their Moslem leaders. It belongs instead to wealthy Christian landlords in Beirut. With the rebellion now ended, these landlords want their land back, for a shore road built by the Lebanese Government in 1959 has brought the beach closer to the city and multiplied the value of the land.

But the squatters are reluctant to leave their little concrete homes; to take down the glass chandeliers with which some of them have decorated their entry halls; to roll up their mattress beds and become rootless again; to abandon their school, their open-air fruit stalls where loudspeakers blare out the voice of Radio Cairo. Above all, the squatters confront grimly any interloper who threatens the settlement's new mosque, whose white minaret is a landmark far down the beach on either side.

Police trying to assert the rights of the landlords have been driven back by stones from the raw, new village in the sands. Not only do the settlers resist evacuation; they demand compensation from the landlord in the event they are forced to leave. After all, the squatters reason, did not their leaders promise them protection?

This problem remains unsolved; and if it finally is resolved, the decision will stem not from the legal niceties of the case, but from the comparative political power which each side—the Christian landlords in their palaces or the Moslem leaders with street mobs under their control —is able to muster.

From almost all foreigners, I suspect, the private thinking of "little" Arabs is veiled. Yet occasionally there are insights which permit even us at least to guess what these people must be thinking.

Our apartment in Beirut stands on a cliff fronting the Mediterranean Sea, and directly below our house a rocky headland juts out from the shore. Sheltered among the rocks of this headland nestles the hut of several Arab fishermen, whose boats are drawn up in the lee of the headland's little cove. Several times a week, as I sit at my desk, I hear the dull boom of an explosion below. If I look up quickly enough, I see a white geyser falling back into the sea, into a widening ring symbolizing death and destruction. The explosion was caused by dynamite, thrown into the water by one of the fishermen. A few moments later he slips naked into the sea, armed with a net, and ignoring the dead fingerlings floating belly upward to the surface, dives for the few larger fish which may have been killed by the blast.

All up and down the coast of Lebanon this happens, and the toll of fish too small to be useful, the food fish of later years, must be enormous. Dynamiting is illegal in Lebanon, but the police cannot be at all places at all times up and down the indented shoreline of the country.

Another day my family and I went to our beach cabin

at Acapulco beach just south of Beirut. Drawn up on the sands was a large double-ended rowing boat, which at dawn had been used to lay a huge fishing net offshore. Now it was ten o'clock, and two lines of men, one for each end of the net, slowly pulled the vast mesh envelope into shore. Each man wore a towel, or old jacket, or other protection wadded at the small of his back. Belted around each man's waist, drawing the wadded protection snug against him, was a piece of rope whose extra length was knotted at the end.

This knotted end each man fastened over the long rope leading down to the net in the sea. Eleven men to the rope pulling one side of the net; an equal number on the other side. Between them stood their captain in khaki shirt and white shorts, exhorting, guiding his men, keeping an anxious eye on the tautened ropes.

Digging in their heels, the lines of men backed slowly across the sands, among the expensive beach cabins of Acapulco beach. As each man reached a certain point in his backward journey, he peeled off the line and ran down toward the surf, there to engage his knotted rope again and lean back for a new pull. One man at a time, always ten men pulling, one man running down the beach to fasten his line again.

So the ropes were maintained always taut, to keep the big net buoy-surfaced at the top and dragging the sandy bottom so that no prey might escape. For half an hour we watched; they had been pulling for at least that long before we came. As the great bulk of the net loomed dark in the water, excitement mounted. The ends of the net itself rose dripping from the surf. Now each man took hold of the net by hand, gathering it inward to anchor men rapidly coiling the folds on the beach.

The moment came. Led by their captain the men rushed

forward into the water, dragged the body of the net into shore, above the reach of the waves. Together they stared down into the meshes. No gleam of silver, no heaving of life against the folds. Perhaps six small fish slightly larger than minnows lay caught in the toils.

Six tiny fish, twenty-three men, including the captain. A morning's work, but no reward. No bread, nor olives, nor fresh cheese for the families in the rude huts scattered throughout the city.

Without a complaint or show of disappointment the men folded their net, picking out the seaweed and debris, tossing away the useless fish. Then, while two men placed rollers beneath the keel and another splashed sea water on the rollers to ease the passage, the fishermen hauled their heavy-timbered boat up the beach, safe above the surf line.

Tomorrow they would try again, at some other place. Carrying their gear they drifted quietly away. After a few moments, the Westerners on the beach who had watched them, some with cameras in hand, went back to their swimming and sunning.

What these men had practiced with their net and boat was legal fishing. Perhaps some of them, when the occasion offered, threw dynamite into the sea. But perhaps they did not. Did they think that morning, as they tramped away from their fruitless work, of the dynamiters whose blasts over the years had contributed directly to their empty net?

The fishermen, farmers, builders, artisans, the nomads in their tents, and the emerging middle class—these, multiplied in their millions, are the peoples of the Middle East, the wealth-producing backbone of Lebanon, Syria, Jordan, Iraq, Egypt, Israel, and Iran.

This book will seem not to be about them, but about their

leaders, the handful of men—kings, presidents, and prime ministers—who make the decisions affecting the lives of the millions. It is these leaders, and not the common people, with whom the governments of the West, including that of the United States, must deal in forging their relations with the Middle East.

The leaders make the moves, but the lives principally affected belong to the "little" people. These people are the raw stuff of the Middle East; difficult, if not impossible, for the Westerner fully to comprehend; slow-moving but malleable, either toward complaisance or sullen explosiveness. They form the background for the events described in this book.

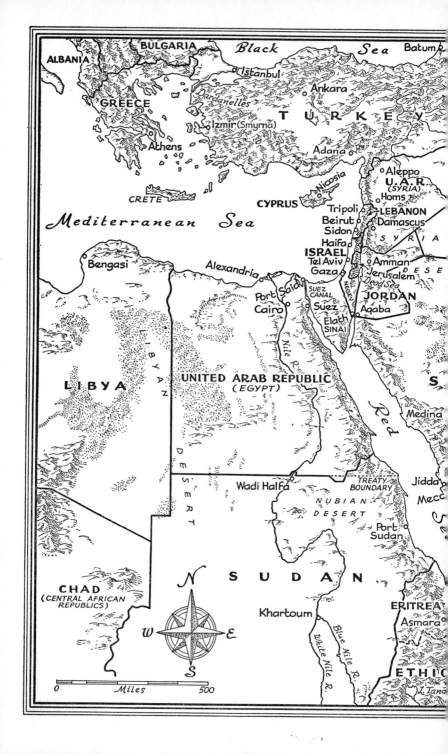

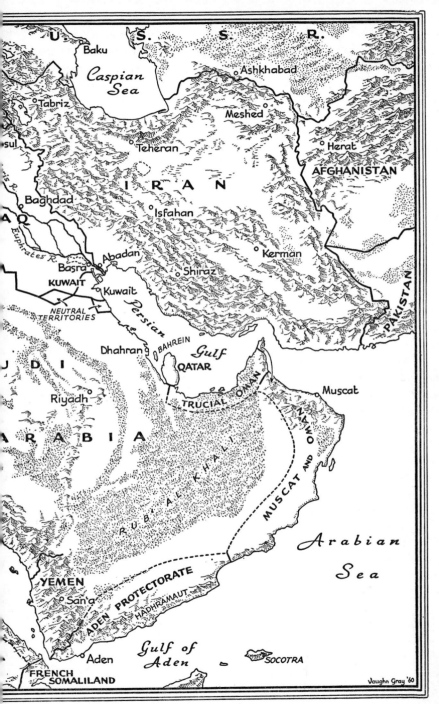

## CHAPTER 2

# "When Communism Enters a Country"

During 1959 two events occurred which shed striking light on the development of President's Nasser's thinking about communism. The first event, which stretched out over a period of several months, began on April 11, 1959, with the publication in Cairo of a booklet entitled "What Happens When Communism Enters a Country." In the first six days after the book was published, it sold more than 100,000 copies—compared with the 10,000 copies which a normal best seller in Egypt might expect to achieve.

The book was paper-bound in bright red. It sold for two piasters—about five cents. It was an exact copy, translated into Arabic and complete with pictures, of a booklet on the Hungarian rebellion originally published by *Life* magazine in 1956. The Arabic version had one feature all its own, an unsigned introduction in Arabic titled "The Story of Every People," meaning that what followed was to be read as the story of every people which fell under Communist rule.

Then, in searing fashion, the introduction indicted communism as a destroyer of freedom. It declared that what had happened in Hungary would happen to any people who were deceived by the red flag, who did not realize that that flag was stained red by the blood of millions of people.

Four months after the publication of the booklet I lunched in Cairo with the man who had published it, Mustafa Amin, co-editor and publisher with his twin brother of the popular Cairo daily, *Al-Akhbar*. (This was before *Al-Akhbar*, together with three other newspaper and magazine publishing houses, were nationalized by the United Arab Republic government.) Three hundred thousand copies of the booklet had been snapped up by Arabs in Egypt, Yemen, the Sudan, Lebanon, Morocco, Libya, and Jordan, Mr. Amin told me. Eight thousand copies had been smuggled into Iraq, where Communists and anti-Communists then were struggling for control of the country, and had been sold on the black market for as much as two dollars each. Copies still were circulating in the North African market at prices up to one dollar apiece.

Letters asking for copies of the booklet had poured into the newspaper's office from points as scattered as Brazil, Chile, Belgium, West Germany, Norway, Pakistan, and Australia. In August, the editor said, the Chinese Communist Foreign Ministry had complained to the United Arab Republic chargé d'affaires in Peking that China was receiving reports from Afro-Asian countries about an anti-Communist book published in Cairo. The Chinese were astonished, the Foreign Ministry spokesman is said to have declared, that the U.A.R. would allow publication of a book unfriendly to the Socialist camp.

"Are you going to print any more?" I asked Mr. Amin. "We have just printed 100,000 new copies," he answered. "But they will not go on sale. Every copy has been taken by the U.A.R. government for distribution to high school and university students in Syria and Egypt."

The meaning of the tale does not end there. In 1956 the United States Information Service produced an exact forerunner of this book, also in Arabic, but printed with a black cover and without a special introduction. The title of the U.S.I.S. version was "The Struggle of Hungary for Freedom." It was not sold—it was given away. But almost no one read it. Why? Because it was regarded by most Arabs who saw it as propaganda put out by the Baghdad Pact powers.

For three years that U.S.I.S. version had been available in the Middle East, including Egypt, and had caused scarcely a ripple of interest. Yet it was the same book, minus the unsigned introduction written in Cairo, as the red-covered version which very likely became the fastest-selling book in recent Middle East history.

From the beginning of the Hungarian rebellion the United States Embassy in Cairo had striven to set the facts of the case before the Egyptian people. But the Hungarian revolt had coincided with the invasion of Egypt by Britain, France, and Israel, and as a consequence anti-Western feeling in Egypt was at its height. The American Embassy got nowhere with its presentation of material on Hungary. Much of its booklet and pamphlet information on the rebellion was scrapped by Egyptian postal authorities before it could be delivered; that which did get through was ignored by the Cairo press. The Hungarian rebellion, and its crushing by the Soviet Army, were not fit subjects for Egyptians to learn about, in the view of the Egyptian government.

Less than three years later the same Egyptian authorities encouraged in every way possible the publication in Arabic of a damning indictment of the Soviet role in Hungary, and even directed that Egyptian and Syrian students should be exposed to the story. Obviously, in those interim months, a distinct change had come over the thinking of President Nasser and his aides.

The second event throwing light on Mr. Nasser's thinking occurred just before the opening of school in the fall of 1959. Mohammed Heykal, editor of the Cairo daily *Al-Ahram*, and a trusted friend of President Nasser, came quietly to the American and Canadian ambassadors and asked them whether their countries, together with Britain, could accept on an urgent basis several hundred U.A.R. students who otherwise would have to go to Communist schools for study. Some of these students already had been studying in the Soviet Union, and Egyptian officials were deeply concerned over the amount of Communist indoctrination they had been absorbing along with their assigned studies.

Most of these students were pursuing postgraduate technical courses, and it was not easy to find places for them in Western universities. The United States was asked to accept about 200, Britain a roughly equal number, and Canada 20 students. All three governments, recognizing this as a clear gain for the free world, set up a crash program, and every one of the students in question was enrolled in the West. Those who went to the United States joined approximately 730 U.A.R. students—300 from Syria and the rest from Egypt—already studying in America, while those who went to British schools joined about 600 of their fellows in Britain. The 20 who went to Canada were the first ever sent to that country at the expense of the Egyptian government.

Not all U.A.R. students were withdrawn from Communist institutions, nor were the public reasons for the switch openly disparaging to the Soviet Union. It was announced in Cairo that Egyptian and Syrian students had had difficulty in learning Russian, and that the disparity between Marxist and U.A.R. theories and practices rendered some of their learning inapplicable at home. All of this was true —but privately the Egyptians left no doubt that their major concern was the Communist orientation some of their students were acquiring in the lands of the Soviet bloc.

One reason for the Egyptian alarm was disclosed in a December 29, 1959, Reuters dispatch datelined Berlin. This report described an "indoctrination school" being run by the East German government in Leipzig for students from Arab, Asian, and African countries. At this "Institute for Foreigners," the report's "authoritative" but unnamed source said, students were given a course in Communist theory and ideology before starting their training in universities and industrial establishments. The course at the school was said to last six months, and included lectures on Marxism-Leninism and the benefits for underdeveloped countries to be derived from communism.

These two events—publication of the anti-Communist booklet and the switch of U.A.R. students from East to West—bore concrete testimony to the Egyptians' growing distrust of the Communist bloc. There is ample evidence of the genuineness and depth of this distrust, both in President Nasser's public words and even more in things which Egyptians have said and done privately in an attempt to blunt the edge of Communist penetration of the U.A.R.

Unequivocal evidence that Mr. Nasser was ready to acknowledge the creeping chilliness between himself and Moscow came in a speech he delivered at Port Said December 23, 1958, when he denounced Arab Communists as "Zionist agents." This illogical charge apparently stemmed from President Nasser's reluctance at that time to offend the Soviet Union in his attack on local Arab Communists. The speech was followed by a drive to arrest all known Communists operating in Syria and Egypt, to seize their clandestine printing presses, and in every way to make it as difficult as possible for Communists to operate in the U.A.R.

Cairo's specific concern resulted from the success Iraqi Communists then were having at infiltrating the movement of Premier Abdel Karim Kassem in Baghdad, and from the fear that Communists might be equally successful in Syria, now the northern province of Mr. Nasser's United Arab Republic, and traditionally the headquarters of Arab communism.

To anyone familiar with Egypt's economic situation it was obvious why Cairo hoped to keep its new campaign against Arab Communists separate and distinct from its relations with the Soviet Union. By this time Egypt had lost its traditional Western markets for Egyptian cotton, and was relying primarily upon the Communist bloc to buy this all-important crop, which furnished 60 per cent of Egypt's foreign exchange income. Furthermore, both the Egyptian and Syrian armies were armed with Communist weapons, while a number of Soviet-financed technical aid projects were in progress in both sectors of the U.A.R. As Mohammed Heykal said to me in Cairo early in January, 1959, Egypt's alliance with the Soviets was, from the Egyptian point of view, a defensive thing. Egypt had little choice but to turn to Moscow, since only the Soviets were willing to furnish what the U.A.R. felt it needed.

Within that same month, however, Mr. Heykal, obviously reflecting President Nasser's views, chided Soviet Premier Nikita S. Khrushchev for talking out of turn. In an article signed by himself as editor of *Al-Ahram*, Mr. Heykal rebuked Mr. Khrushchev for criticizing the U.A.R. for its suppression of Arab Communists. This the Soviet Premier had done in a speech before the twenty-first Soviet Communist Party Congress in Moscow January 27, when he declared it was wrong to accuse Communists, as the leaders of the U.A.R. were doing, of "working against national efforts in the struggle against imperialism."[1]

Accusing Mr. Khrushchev of meddling in the U.A.R.'s internal affairs, Mr. Heykal reminded the Soviet Premier of the latter's own declaration that Stalin, Malenkov, Beria, Kaganovitch, and Bulganin had betrayed their party's trust in them. Therefore, Mr. Heykal affirmed, it was incorrect to say—as Khrushchev had done—that Communists could not be accused of working against national efforts.

This was the beginning of a war of words, and the spring of 1959 was characterized by increasingly harsh recriminations between Moscow and Cairo. On March 16 Mr. Khrushchev accused Nasser of "adopting the language of the imperialists" in condemning Arab Communists and the Kassem regime in Iraq, and added that the U.A.R. would like to annex Iraq to itself.[2] These comments were given additional sting because they were delivered at the signing of a Soviet-Iraqi economic agreement in Moscow. Replying in Damascus the next day, President Nasser

[1] *The Christian Science Monitor*, January 30, 1959. *New York Times*, January 29, 1959.
[2] *The Christian Science Monitor*, March 17, 1959.

scorned the charge that the U.A.R. wanted to annex Iraq, and accused Mr. Khrushchev of distorting the facts.

Two days later the Soviet leader described Nasser as a "rather hotheaded young man" who "took upon himself more than his stature permitted" in attacking the Iraqi and other Arab Communists.[3] Retorting that his "hot-headedness" had succeeded in ridding Egypt of imperialist control, Nasser never slackened his drumfire of attacks against the Communists of Iraq.

In an interview he granted to the Indian journalist R. K. Karanjia, in April, 1959, President Nasser disclosed something of the origins of his new attitude toward international communism. In that interview Mr. Nasser declared the U.A.R. had uncovered a Communist conspiracy to create a Soviet state in Iraq, from which the Communists would work to wreck the Syrian-Egyptian union, and then go on to establish a Communist "fertile crescent" comprising Iraq, Syria, Jordan, Lebanon, and Kuwait. By this means, Nasser indicated, the Soviet Union would be able to gain access to the Persian Gulf, the Gulf of Aqaba, and the Indian Ocean. Referring to Communist activities in Iraq, Mr. Nasser exclaimed: "We are like one Arab family in a boat in storm-tossed seas. . . . If someone tries to drill a hole under us, can you expect us to sit silently and watch the catastrophe?"[4]

All this was not allowed to lead to a final break between Moscow and Cairo, and by late May of 1959 both Nasser and Khrushchev—each impelled by his own considerations—had realized the wisdom of at least a surface patching up of relations between them. On May 21 *Al-Ahram* referred to an interview which Mr. Karanjia had recently had with

[3] *New York Times*, March 19, 1959.
[4] *Egyptian Mail*, April 18, 1959.

Khrushchev in Moscow, during which the Soviet Premier had declared that the people of the United Arab Republic had no more sincere and true friend than Russia.

In its editorial of May 21, *Al-Ahram*, again obviously reflecting President Nasser's desires, wrote:

> We accept Khrushchev's words with their full meaning. We accept the friendship he reaffirms. And we sincerely forget everything that happened March 16 (the day Khrushchev accused Nasser of using the language of the imperialists). We hope that our relations will be back to normal now that the cloud has been dissipated by Khrushchev's friendly remarks.[5]

In this way Cairo stopped the public exchange of recriminations for fear that the entire system of Soviet technical and economic aid to the U.A.R. would crumble, leaving Egypt and Syria bereft of Russian aid, and uncertain whether or not the West would fill the vacuum. Behind the scenes, however, the relationship between Nasser and Khrushchev remained coldly distrustful. This is not speculation, but is borne out by known facts.

On April 20, 1959, in the midst of their quarrel, Mr. Khrushchev had sent President Nasser a lengthy personal letter, which never has been published. The Soviet leader began the letter with a long review of history, justifying "legitimate" Russian interests in the Middle East, yet asserting that never had the Soviet Union acted in an imperialistic manner in securing those interests. The West, on the other hand, had acted imperialistically vis-à-vis the Arabs, and had taken the side of Israel.

Mr. Khrushchev went on to say that he still respected the U.A.R.'s positive neutrality and was willing to recognize President Nasser as leader of Arab nationalism in

[5] *Al-Ahram*, May 21, 1959.

most of the Middle East. But—and this was the crucial part of the letter—Iraq must be allowed to work out its own destiny, and Nasser was reminded that Iraq was not wholly an Arab nation. This referred to the Kurds of Iraq, almost one-quarter of the total population, whom the Soviets consistently have sought to make an instrument of Communist expansion.

This part of the letter deeply disturbed Nasser, since it confirmed his suspicion that Moscow intended to concentrate on Iraq as a base for Communist penetration of the Middle East. Still, he felt, his own situation in this respect would not be improved but rendered more shaky if the U.A.R. were to cut off economic relations with the Soviet Union. And Nasser hoped that once Moscow became convinced that the Nasser-led movement of Arab nationalism was stronger than Arab communism, the Soviets would have no choice but to cooperate with him.

In his reply, delivered in Moscow May 22, 1959, Mr. Nasser is believed to have agreed to the terms of "truce" which the Soviet Premier had proposed. "Truce" in fact is an inaccurate word. Rather the two leaders had laid down certain limits within which their contest of strength would continue. The stake in this struggle was either the eventual supremacy of an Iraq-based Communist movement in the Middle East or President Nasser's unchallenged position as leader of Arab nationalism in the entire eastern Arab world. In the meantime both the Soviets and Egyptians felt it to be to their mutual benefit to continue economic and technical aid relations.

Since that time President Nasser has been under no illusions concerning the direction of Soviet policy in the Middle East. His intelligence service has informed him that the Soviets, in promising to make the Iraqi Air Force the best in the Arab world, also assured Iraqi Premier Kassem that his archenemy, Nasser, would not receive the most modern Soviet weapons. It is a fact that by spring of 1960 the supply of Communist arms to the U.A.R. had dwindled to a trickle of spare parts and replacements. In particular Mr. Nasser had been unable to obtain the MIG-19 jet fighters which he felt he must have to match the late model Super Mystères which Israel had received from France and the even more modern Mirage III aircraft which France agreed to sell Israel in the summer of 1960.

This continuing inner disturbance on the part of U.A.R. leaders was largely masked from the Egyptian and Syrian public. When Salah Salem, formerly a Nasser aide and now editor of the government-owned Cairo newspaper *Al-Gomhouriya*, visited Moscow in November, 1959, he wrote of his cordial welcome by Khrushchev, and of Khrushchev's friendly greetings to Nasser. In private Major Salem told another story when he returned to Cairo. He informed President Nasser that Mr. Khrushchev's attitude had been tough and unyielding, and that the Soviet leader had made clear Moscow's intention of supporting the Iraqi regime of General Kassem. Furthermore, Salem reported, Khrushchev had said he did not approve of Mr. Nasser's attitude, and that even if the U.A.R. obtained MIG-19 fighters to match Israel's French planes, it would have to pay the full price for them.

President Nasser's estimate of Communist intentions is believed to have convinced him that the Soviets are prepared to play a long and unspectacular game in the Middle East, aimed primarily at preparing Iraq as a base of operations for Communist expansion in the area and at undermining the position of Nasser among the Arabs. This campaign is expected to continue whether or not Premier

Kassem remains in power in Iraq, so long as the present climate for Communist activities prevails in Baghdad. Should a future anti-Communist government in Baghdad succeed in driving the Communists wholly underground, Moscow's strategy would have to be revised.

As Cairo sees it, the Soviet Union has no present desire to see Iraqi Communists assume total administrative responsibility for governing Iraq but is satisfied with the restoration of legal political life in the country, within which framework the Communists hope to solidify their control of key government operations. Primary Communist goals appear to be control of the ministries of education and of national guidance (propaganda), including control of Baghdad Radio and domination of the Iraqi press, and direction of the land reform administration.

While Iraqi Communists seek control of key government posts, the Soviet Union itself will work on the government-to-government level with Iraq, giving military and economic aid, much as it did and to some extent still does with the U.A.R. To the Chinese Communists will be left the "activist" task of guiding the policies of the Iraqi Communist Party. On occasion the Soviets may even inform Iraqi officials that Moscow "deplores" the work of the Chinese among street Communists, thereby hoping to persuade doubtful Iraqi authorities that the Communists in Iraq are divided and uncertain.

This, it should be understood, is the Egyptian theory of how the Communists plan to operate in Iraq. Evidence available to Western experts indicates that the Egyptian position may be essentially correct. The great unknown element in the equation is whether the Chinese have adopted their more activist role in agreement or disagreement with the Soviets.

Twice during 1959, at policy discussion meetings in eastern Europe, the Chinese and Soviets are believed to have disagreed on tactics to be pursued by the Communists in underdeveloped nations. The Soviets are said to have emphasized the importance of Communist economic aid programs to these lands with the goal of increasing their dependence on the Sino-Soviet bloc. This gradualist approach characterizes Soviet programs in Afghanistan, the U.A.R., and Iraq.

The Chinese, however, are believed to have argued for the direct fomentation of revolutions in underdeveloped lands through Communist control, where possible, of trade unions, student and other popular groups, enlisted ranks of the army, and ultimately street mobs. The Chinese reportedly insisted on the primacy of Peking in providing Communist leadership in Asia.

Whatever resolution of these alleged differences may or may not have been made, the Chinese and Soviets in Iraq appear to be following out their separate convictions. In the spring of 1960 the New China News Agency (Hsinhua) had twenty-seven staff members in Baghdad, compared with a more modest bureau for Tass, the Soviet news agency. Twenty-seven Chinese reporters were hardly necessary to cover news developments in Iraq.

Shortly after the Iraqi revolution in 1958 a Chinese Moslem named Burhan Shahidi appeared in Baghdad. This man had been active in Cairo at the time the U.A.R. recognized Communist China diplomatically in 1956. As Egyptian distrust of the Chinese gradually deepened, Shahidi fell under Cairo's suspicion as a leading organizer of Peking's propaganda and, presumably, espionage activities in the U.A.R.

When he arrived in Baghdad, Shahidi was instrumental in organizing the Chinese-Iraqi Friendship Society, as he had been earlier in forming the Chinese-Egyptian Friendship Society. To these tasks Mr. Shahidi brought not only his Islamic faith but also a fluent knowledge of Arabic.

The Egyptians believe Shahidi helped to instigate violent Communist tactics in Iraq at the time of the Mosul revolt and Kirkuk massacre in the spring and summer of 1959, when Iraqi Communists tried to terrorize Iraq by dragging anti-Communist Iraqis through the streets. Following the Kirkuk uprising in July, 1959, Iraqi security officials captured Communist maps in which the homes of leading anti-Communists in Baghdad had been marked with an "x" to indicate which persons were to be dragged through the streets when the opportunity arose.

Perhaps even the Chinese were embarrassed by Col. Fadhel Abbas Mahdawi, pro-Communist President of the notorious People's Court in Baghdad. One day when a delegation of Chinese Communists was visiting his court, Mahdawi informed his TV and radio audience that his guests had expressed regret the Chinese revolution had preceded that of Iraq. Otherwise, Mahdawi asserted, the Chinese said they could have used the Iraqi tactic of street dragging.

Soviet purposes very likely are served by having the Chinese coordinate the usually clandestine activities of local Communist parties, leaving Moscow free to work "respectably" at the government-to-government level. Because Soviet purposes are thus served, it is hard to know whether agreement or disagreement prevailed in assignment of Communist roles in Iraq.

As part of this general pattern of Communist activity, the Communist parties of surrounding Middle Eastern lands are believed to have moved their headquarters into Iraq. The Tudeh (Communist) Party of Iran appears currently to be centered at the Iraqi towns of Suleimaniyah and Basra, both close to the Iranian frontier. The Jordanian Communist Party likewise is reported to have headquarters in Iraq, at the towns of Najaf and Kerbala. Syrian and Turkish Communists are believed to be centering their activities at the northern Iraqi city of Mosul. In each case the headquarters is placed within easy communication of the neighboring country most directly concerned.

Outside Iraq the Communists, operating wherever possible through trade unions, students', teachers', and other professional associations, and leftist political groups, will seek to show that any economic failures within the U.A.R. result from the lingering control which conservatives will be said to exercise in Cairo and Damascus. Such failures will be contrasted with the "successes" being achieved by Iraq. It will be pointed out that American "imperialism" has replaced that of the British and French, and that the U.A.R. is proving particularly susceptible to the siren call of United States aid. Although Arab unity will be endorsed publicly by the Communists because it must be, the present tendencies of this movement—i.e., the merger of Egypt and Syria—will be described as a vehicle for Egyptian expansionism under Nasser.

While all this is going on, the Soviet Union, apparently disinterested and friendly, will be earnestly engaged in helping whatever Arab lands desire aid in improving their internal living standards. Thus Soviet help in building Egypt's High Aswan Dam in no way conflicts with the Communists' desire to tarnish the name of President Nasser among the Arabs. Indeed, Soviet economic aid to underdeveloped Arab lands will be strenuously promoted in the hope it will minimize anti-Communist efforts on the part of Arab nationalists.

Another area in which Egyptian suspicions of the Communists have been aroused is the so-called Afro-Asian People's Solidarity Council, ostensibly a nongovernmental consultative body set up in Cairo in December, 1957. At the time it was established Western observers suspected it might become an organ for Communist subversion throughout Africa as well as the Middle East. This suspicion was heightened when the Soviet Union, though it had not attended the earlier Bandung conference which foreshadowed the Cairo organization, was specifically invited by Egypt to become a member of the Afro-Asian People's Solidarity Council in Cairo.

The day-to-day work of this council is handled by a permanent secretariat based in Cairo, consisting of a secretary-general and ten secretaries. Among this group the Soviet, Chinese Communist, and Egyptian (later United Arab Republic) secretaries play a leading role. Until the beginning of 1959, these secretaries worked in concert, with the U.A.R. apparently convinced that the African aims of Egypt, the Soviet Union, and Communist China were all directed toward ridding the African continent of colonialism.

Early in 1959, just as President Nasser's distrust of the Communists was coming into focus, the Egyptians became disturbed by the sedulous wooing and indoctrination of young African leaders by the two Communist powers in the Afro-Asian group. Among other things, the Soviet Union and Communist China were using the Afro-Asian body as a channel to invite young Africans to visit Communist lands and even study there. In these Africans U.A.R. officials saw possible future leaders of Africa's emerging nations. Adding to this concern was Cairo's disquiet at Peking's financial and moral backing of the Algerian nationalists fighting for independence from France, a cause which hitherto Cairo had considered peculiarly its own.

This combination of factors produced a split early in 1959 between the U.A.R. secretary and his Communist colleagues. Tension was heightened in February, 1959, when Communist members pushed through a ruling that subsequent matters before the secretariat would be decided by majority vote. From that point on, the U.A.R. secretary found himself consistently outvoted, partly because several seats on the secretariat were vacant and partly because at least two other members of the group were sympathetic to the Soviet Union and Communist China. As a result, President Nasser—very likely ruing the day he invited the Soviets to join the organization—is believed to have appealed to the nations concerned to send genuine neutrals rather than pro-Communists to fill the vacant seats on the secretariat.

Even in the economic realm, the highly touted area of U.A.R.-Soviet cooperation, Cairo and Damascus have found specific reason to be distressed. They have learned that, although the Communists were paying premium prices for Egyptian cotton and Syrian wheat, artificially high price tags had been attached to the goods which the Soviets bartered in return. Experience also showed that Communist deliveries often were slow in coming, and that the quality and even type of product finally delivered sometimes differed from the specifications originally agreed upon. Yet, since Syria and Egypt already had delivered the commodities which had paid for the defective Communist goods, it was difficult to obtain redress.

In some fields, notably missile and rocket development and space research, the Soviets remain ahead of the best the West so far has offered. But it is equally true that in many areas of general manufacture, Communist goods are inferior to the Western products to which the Arabs had become accustomed. Among items about which U.A.R. spokesmen specifically complained were Hungarian locomotives, Soviet trucks, East German automobiles, other Communist-bloc steel products, the high sulphur content of Soviet crude oil, and the presence of foreign matter in some shipments of Russian wheat sent to Egypt.

Another item of considerable annoyance to the Egyptians is the fact that the Soviet Union and Czechoslovakia resell some of their Egyptian cotton at discount prices on the free world market. At one time it was possible for a Western European buyer to purchase a shipment of cotton from the Russians before the cotton even had left Egypt. Instead of moving to its consigned Soviet port, the cotton would be taken to a port like Trieste and from there transshipped to its Western buyer. Although it is difficult to obtain accurate figures on the amount of Egyptian cotton resold by the Communists, it is known that West Germany pays the Soviet bloc about $25,000,000 annually for Egyptian cotton, because it can get the cotton cheaper that way than from Egypt directly.

The reality of the U.A.R. President's distrust of the Communists can no longer be reasonably doubted. To believe that this distrust eventually may melt away merely because Nasser once was naive about the Communists would be to disregard the hard lessons he has learned since he signed his Soviet arms deal in 1955. This does not mean that the U.A.R. can easily disengage itself from that economic dependence upon the Soviet bloc into which it has sunk since 1955. The extent of that dependence, which will be analyzed subsequently, is enormous.

It does seem clear, however, that President Nasser's future dealings with Moscow will be carried on with the knowledge that the Soviets aim eventually at his denigration or destruction. This conviction on his part has not suddenly transformed Mr. Nasser into an ally of the West, since he remains perhaps equally suspicious of Western, principally British and French, motives in the Middle East. But his developing awareness of Communist intentions is causing him to reappraise basically his relationship with at least one Western nation, the United States. It is that reappraisal, coupled with an equally frank and sometimes painful American re-estimate of President Nasser, that has opened the way to improved Arab-American relations.

# CHAPTER 3

# Cairo Through Washington's Eyes

American thinking toward President Nasser indirectly was conditioned by the Palestine war of 1948, long before most officers of the State Department had heard of the Egyptian colonel. Outright American support of the Zionists in the period leading up to the creation of the Jewish state had cost the United States heavily in the Arab world. By the time Israel was established and the Arab-Jewish war had been fought, the United States government had become an enemy in Arab eyes.

The State Department had been amply forewarned of this reaction by its diplomats in the field. George Wadsworth, while he was American Ambassador to Iraq, had cabled Washington to the effect that American support of the Zionists would cause the loss of the Middle East to the Russians within ten years. Forty-eight hours after Mr. Wadsworth's cable was sent, every American ambassador, minister, and consul general in the area had endorsed it or sent similar views of their own. Theirs was not an expression of anti-Semitism, nor a moral judgment of the issues involved, but a professional assessment of what American diplomats believed Arab reaction to U.S. policy would be, and the damaging effect this would have over the long run on American interests in Asia and Africa.

Alarmed by the mounting strength of this anti-Ameriman feeling, American diplomats throughout the Middle East were seeking out "reasonable" Arab leaders, capable of coming to terms with Israel and settling the Arab-Jewish quarrel. Early in 1949 this search coincided in Damascus with the pretensions to power of the chief of staff of the Syrian Army, Col. Husni Zaim.

For some time Colonel Zaim had been sounding out members of the United States Legation in Damascus concerning a plan he had in mind. That plan was to overthrow the civilian government of Syria and replace it with an Army regime headed by himself. Zaim and his fellow Army officers had been embittered by the attempts of the Syrian government, headed by President Shukri el-Kuwatly, to blame the Syrian Army for Syria's poor showing in the Arab-Jewish war. Zaim contended this poor showing stemmed from corruption and inefficiency in the government in Damascus, which had undercut the efforts of the Army in the field. His solution was a clean-cut Army *coup d'état* that would purge the body politic and allow a fresh start to be made.

Whether to his surprise or not, Colonel Zaim met an encouraging response from the Americans he contacted. He then set about fabricating rumors that would cause foreign diplomatic missions to believe that security was at a low state in Syria, and that foreigners were actually in physical danger. "Informed circles" in Syria were led to believe that the Kurds in northern Syria were on the verge of revolt and that the Kurds in Damascus were harboring dangerous Communist agents. Confidentially he informed the American, French, and British legations that the Communists had prepared an assassination list including, besides his own name and that of President Kuwatly, the names of the American, French, and British ministers. By these means Zaim sought to create tension so that his efforts to position his troops in preparation for a *coup d'état* would appear natural.

On March 30, 1949, Zaim capitalized on his manufactured incidents to seize power in a bloodless coup. President Kuwatly and his civilian government were deposed. The United States hoped that a "reasonable" Arab leader now had been found, strong enough to stand out against mob pressures and to help settle the Palestine problem. These hopes were short-lived. Six months after he had seized power the "field marshal," as Zaim had restyled himself, was killed in a new *coup d'état* launched by Col. Sami Hinnawi. Zaim, according to Hinnawi, had become a dictator and had failed to move toward promised social and economic reforms. Hinnawi lasted even less time than his predecessor. In December, 1949, Hinnawi was ousted in a policy quarrel by Lt. Col. Adib Shishakly.

The Syrian stage had become crowded by a shifting kaleidoscope of Army officers, who tended to be as self-seeking as the politicians whom they had replaced. Despite considerable public sentiment for union of Syria with Iraq, the Syrian Army scotched the plan chiefly because its officer corps would have been swallowed up by the larger and more powerful Iraqi Army. More serious from Washington's point of view was the increasing use of

Israel as a whipping boy by Syrian officers scrambling for position and power.

Clearly American intervention in Syria had failed to produce a leader who could help the United States out of its impasse over Palestine. But within the State Department hope lingered that such an Arab leader eventually would come to light. This hope remained an important element in Washington's thinking in July, 1952, when an Egyptian Army junta overthrew King Farouk and State Department eyes first fastened on Lt. Col. Gamal Abdel Nasser.

American contacts with Colonel Nasser began in an unorthodox way. Even before the revolution certain American diplomats and private individuals, realizing that the deteriorating Egyptian situation might have grave implications for United States interests, had made contact with Colonel Nasser and other members of his Army group. Cool to these approaches, Nasser made it clear that whatever he decided to do would be an independent move and that he would not be a party to any "imperialist plot." Nasser insisted he would do "what was good for Egypt, regardless of whether or not it fitted into the plans of one or another of the Great Powers." In later days Colonel Nasser was to repeat this statement time and again to various foreign diplomats, Western and Russian, who tried to influence him.

Nonetheless, the Americans were impressed by Colonel Nasser's forthrightness and intelligence, and they regarded his determination to act independently and his refusal to discuss his plans and make commitments as good signs. At least they were convinced this man was no Zaim, who had actively sought out Western help.

One important result of these early contacts was the development of personal friendships between Colonel Nasser and a few Americans who were officially or privately concerned with Egyptian affairs. One of them was William Lakeland, then Second Secretary of the American Embassy in Cairo, who had met Nasser socially. Another was Kermit Roosevelt, grandson of President Theodore Roosevelt, who had had much experience in the Middle East as writer and lecturer, and who was at the time a special assistant to the Secretary of State. Others were members of the American management-consulting teams who were in Egypt working for private Egyptian industrial and business organizations.

Though none of these individuals attained any degree of influence over Nasser—as "foreign advisers" were supposed to have had over King Farouk in the days of British occupation—their informal relationships with the Egyptian colonel permitted an exchange of ideas rarely possible between Westerners and the leader of an Eastern country.

Meanwhile, Colonel Nasser was beginning to move toward the public leadership of the revolution which in fact he had headed from the beginning. He first had emerged into general public notice in January, 1953. At that time, as acting chief of staff of the Army, he had disclosed the arrest on political charges of twenty-five officers and fifteen civilians, the suppression of six Communist newspapers, and the government's intention to arrest every known Communist in Egypt.

On May 18 Nasser moved further into the limelight when he received the title of Vice President of the Revolutionary Command Council, as the thirteen-man Army junta called itself. One month later Nasser took his next step forward by becoming Deputy Premier and Minister of Interior of the Egyptian government under Maj. Gen.

Mohammed Naguib, who held the two posts of President and Prime Minister.

The Americans whom Nasser had met informally played an important role in settling the then outstanding problems between the United States and Egypt. Though Colonel Nasser had great respect for Jefferson Caffrey, the American Ambassador, he found ordinary diplomatic exchanges difficult and felt that in official government-to-government talks he was forced to take a formal and inflexible line. Thus, while Nasser's officials negotiated with Mr. Caffrey on such questions as American economic, technical, and military aid, Colonel Nasser himself exchanged ideas with those Americans who were his personal friends.

Moreover, it was through informal talks with his American friends, principally Kermit Roosevelt, that Nasser eventually worked out a realistic policy for the achievement of his first major foreign policy goal, evacuation of the British from the Suez Canal Zone. When the British and Egyptians signed the evacuation agreement in Cairo on July 27, 1954, it contained some provisions not completely satisfactory to either side. But it is almost certain that no agreement at all would have been possible had it not been for the informal participation of Nasser's American friends.

When Nasser was a young officer planning his revolution, he knew and thought a great deal about Britain, but he knew very little about the United States. What little he did know inclined him to believe that the U.S. was the one great power with which Egypt could deal on a basis of independence. After the revolution Nasser looked toward the United States for help in making his country economically healthy. Colonel Nasser required only that Egypt be left free to make her political decisions alone, and he believed the U.S. would have no objection to this requirement. In particular he insisted that Egypt must remain independent of big power blocs. This was the genesis of his "positive neutrality," a theme later picked up and trumpeted by Cairo Radio and the Egyptian press.

Even when Secretary of State John Foster Dulles was asking nations to "stand up and be counted" on the issue of communism, Nasser could not believe this meant the U.S. would give Egypt economic aid only if Nasser joined what he regarded essentially as a foreign effort against a foreign enemy. He attributed these utterances to the Secretary's personal crusade against communism, or to the pressure of public opinion in the United States. Information Nasser was receiving from his Embassy in Washington, coupled with what he knew from day-to-day dealings between his government and the American Embassy in Cairo, led him to believe he should not take Mr. Dulles' position too seriously, and that there was no reason the United States and Egypt could not cooperate.

On February 27, 1955, Henry A. Byroade arrived in Cairo to replace Jefferson Caffrey as American Ambassador. General Byroade, who had enjoyed a brilliant military career and who had been Assistant Secretary of State for Near East and African Affairs, long had been aware of Nasser's impatience with normal diplomatic procedures. He came to Cairo prepared to meet Nasser on Nasser's terms and to capitalize on the fact that he and Nasser were roughly of the same age, and were both military men. ("I am not a diplomat, but just a soldier," Byroade was fond of saying to Nasser in their early meetings.)

Immediately upon arriving in Cairo Mr. Byroade established excellent informal relations with Mr. Nasser, and before long they had begun calling each other by first name. Mr. Byroade is the only American Ambassador who has dealt with Nasser on this basis. Both Mr. Caffrey and Raymond A. Hare, who succeeded Mr. Byroade, dealt with President Nasser on a basis of mutual respect, but were formal in personal relations.

Through this period Colonel Nasser's personal star had continued to rise within Egypt. During a protracted test of strength with General Naguib in the winter and spring of 1954, Nasser had briefly assumed the premiership, surrendered it to Naguib, and finally had taken the post for good on April 18, 1954. In November of the same year the split between the two men caused Naguib to be placed under house arrest, on charges of plotting with Communists and Moslem Brotherhood extremists against Nasser. Prime Minister Nasser took over presidential duties, though he did not formally assume the title of President until June 23, 1956, following a national plebiscite to elect a President and approve Egypt's new Constitution. At that time the position of prime minister was abolished.

Until Secretary Dulles and the British proposed the Baghdad Pact at the beginning of 1955, American-Egyptian relations went relatively smoothly, with the United States beginning to extend the economic aid which Mr. Nasser sought and needed. Publicly, since the beginning of his visible assumption of power, Nasser had lashed out at the West, including the United States, whenever he felt his "positive neutrality" was being subjected to pressure. Thus it was that the image of an anti-Western Nasser began to rise among the peoples of the West.

Yet Mr. Nasser privately continued to believe that in the long run certain "fundamental American principles," as he termed them, would govern the attitude of the United States toward Egypt. This attitude would permit some kind of mutually profitable relationship to be worked out which would not violate his concept of "positive neutrality." In his relations with Ambassador Byroade Mr. Nasser continued to show flexibility in his desire to cooperate with the United States.

Gradually, however, Mr. Nasser became disillusioned with this view. He began to believe that the U.S. government—at least so long as Mr. Dulles remained in office—would not respect his neutralism unless all other Arab states imposed the same conditions on the U.S. He became convinced that his bargaining power was weak so long as other Arab governments could make "end runs" around him to Washington, and that Egypt's "positive neutrality" was meaningless unless the same position were adopted by other Arab states.

Impelled by the desire to keep other Arab states from joining foreign pacts that might isolate Egypt, Nasser ordered his newly-enlarged Radio Cairo to beam out "anti-imperialist" propaganda designed to make Arab peoples everywhere oppose actions by their governments which might be interpreted as conniving with the imperialists. His success was immediate, and almost overnight Mr. Nasser found himself in the role of an Arab rather than merely an Egyptian leader.

Americans who have known him from the beginning agree that at this time Nasser began to think of himself as a "champion of the little Arabs." It was Nasser's supposed intrigues in other Arab states which began the deterioration of American-Egyptian relations. Mr. Dulles was convinced that Egyptian agents were intriguing to embarrass or overthrow the pro-Western governments of Lebanon, Iraq, and Jordan. President Nasser was convinced that the United States government was encouraging Iraqi Premier

Nuri es-Said, King Hussein of Jordan, and President Chamoun of Lebanon to adopt frankly anti-Nasser positions, and that American agents were actually planning a *coup d'état* to install an anti-Nasser government in Syria.

Both sides, it appears, were taking positions more extreme than evidence available at the time warranted. To American friends, Nasser argued that Cairo Radio was the only instrument he was using to reach Arab peoples. Pro-Nasser groups in the various countries, he insisted, were not organized by Egyptian agents, but were formed locally to serve local political aims. (In this connection, one of Nasser's senior associates once said to the Egyptian leader: "These self-appointed priests of Nasserism in other Arab countries are a constant source of embarrassment to us. We would be better off if we chose our own supporters rather than allow them to choose themselves.")

President Nasser seemed incapable of understanding that American intrigues on the scale he envisioned were virtually impossible to the United States government and that, moreover, a fairly high percentage of American diplomats in the Middle East were not entirely unsympathetic to Nasser's aims.

Until early 1955 the Palestine problem appeared to have occupied a relatively minor place in Mr. Nasser's thinking. He had followed a policy of keeping tension with Israel low. Those Americans who know him well believe that for a long time after his revolution he made a conscientious effort to keep guerrilla raids from Gaza into Israel at the minimum consistent with Arab public opinion. In the winter of 1954-55 two events occurred to alter this situation radically. Unfortunately, they coincided with the establishment of the Baghdad Pact, which finally convinced Mr. Nasser that Secretary Dulles was his personal enemy.

The first event was the trial in Cairo of thirteen Jews charged with spying for Israel. Two of the thirteen were tried *in absentia*, having escaped during the roundup of the others. On Jan. 27, 1955, the Supreme Military Tribunal of Egypt made public its sentences—two of the Jews had been sentenced to death, others to hard labor for terms ranging up to life, and two had been acquitted. On January 31 the two Jews condemned to death as spies were hanged in Cairo.

During this trial various prominent Westerners—British, French, and American—who were sympathetic to President Nasser warned him that Israeli feelings were being strongly roused by the plight of the Jewish accused. Serious troubles from the direction of Israel surely would follow if the spies were hanged. Nasser took the position that the accused would have a fair trial. Beyond that he could or would do nothing, since, after all, the men had been charged with spying, an offense carrying the death penalty in many countries of the world. If the court found the men guilty, they must pay the penalty. A French lawyer permitted by Nasser to attend the trial testified afterward to its fairness.

The second event, impelled by Egyptian guerrilla raids from Gaza and possibly by the Cairo trial, was an attack in March, 1955, by Israeli Army units against Egyptian positions in Gaza. Thirty-eight Egyptian soldiers were killed. This attack shocked Nasser deeply. By his own admission, he realized that henceforth a "soft" policy toward Israel would endanger his position as an Arab leader.

Shortly after the Gaza raid Mr. Nasser intensified his appeals to the United States government for military aid. He asked first to buy $100,000,000 worth, but progressively scaled down his request until the total was in the neighborhood of $20,000,000. The American Embassy in Cairo, realizing that the amount of arms which could be bought for this sum would not enable the Egyptian Army to defeat Israel, strongly favored the arms sale. The Embassy was convinced that Nasser wanted the arms primarily to improve the morale of his troops and to counter growing unrest in the Army. Negotiations dragged on through the spring and summer of 1955. Neither Mr. Nasser nor Ambassador Byroade could obtain a definite answer from Washington.

In July Mr. Byroade made a final appeal to the Department of State, urging that favorable action be taken on the Egyptian request. He suggested that, should Nasser not get this comparatively small amount of arms, he would be forced either to seek arms elsewhere or risk the disaffection of his officers. In the end, negotiations broke down on the minor point of whether Cairo would pay for the weapons in dollars or Egyptian pounds.

Toward the end of these negotiations the Soviet Ambassador offered arms to Egypt in huge quantities—something like five times the amount under discussion with the Americans—and without conditions. Nasser told the American Ambassador of the offer (his doing so was interpreted as blackmail by Washington), but he let only a few key members of his own government in on the secret. Despite this care, Egyptian Army leaders were quick to learn from the Foreign Ministry that Nasser had an opportunity to secure badly needed arms, but that he was stalling because he wanted to retain friendship with the Americans. This reason was almost totally incomprehensible to these officers. They took the view that the United States was the friend of Israel, and the Soviets had taken the side of the Arabs. Egypt should, the officers felt, accept the Soviet offer.

Nonetheless, Nasser stalled from July to September before deciding he could no longer put off accepting the Soviet offer. Before doing so, however, he informed Kermit Roosevelt of his dilemma and indicated he was still open to suggestions as to how he could avoid accepting the arms. Roosevelt had little advice to offer Nasser beyond suggesting that the Egyptian leader could use his new burst of popularity—which both Roosevelt and Nasser foresaw would result from the arms deal—to make some peaceful gesture toward Israel. Although talk of outright peace with Israel was out of the question, it was conceivable that some measures to "reduce the tensions"—measures which might lead to more concrete steps later—could be taken safely by Mr. Nasser.

Roosevelt's discussions with Nasser continued over a period of three days, during which time two events threw the discussions off course. First, news of the arms deal leaked to the outside world just as Mr. Nasser was considering how he himself might control the release. The Soviets had assured him, Nasser told Roosevelt, that the arms deal would remain secret until such time as Cairo chose to disclose it. Mr. Roosevelt pointed out that it was to the advantage of the Soviets to "leak" the news in such a way as to gain maximum disruptive effect in the outside world, and that Nasser certainly could not count on the Soviet promise in this regard.

Mr. Roosevelt turned out to be right. At the very moment he and Nasser were discussing the problem on the third floor of the Revolutionary Command Council headquarters, the phone rang to announce that the British Ambassador wanted an appointment "urgently." When the Ambassador arrived, Mr. Nasser excused himself. A few minutes later, he returned to tell Roosevelt that the British

Ambassador had heard of the arms deal from "confidential sources" and wanted to know if it were true.

However the British had learned the news—from Egyptian officers, from a deliberate Soviet leak, or from other sources—the cat now was out of the bag. Nasser resolved to move ahead by twenty-four hours his announcement of the arms deal and to explain it to the outside world as a matter of defensive necessity in view of recent Israeli attacks along Egypt's borders. But this plan was changed by a second event.

Literally minutes before Nasser was to set out for the auditorium where he would announce the arms deal, an Associated Press report was received saying that George V. Allen, then Assistant Secretary of State for Near Eastern and African Affairs, was being sent to Cairo to give Nasser an "ultimatum" outlining serious consequences for Egypt if Cairo accepted the Soviet arms deal. Among these consequences was the threat of American economic warfare against Egypt.

This second development not only undermined Mr. Roosevelt's efforts, but threw the American Embassy in Cairo into consternation. As Ambassador Byroade and his key officers saw it, Mr. Nasser was doing the best he could under the circumstances and Roosevelt was making progress in exploring the extremely sensitive question of reducing tensions with Israel. Moreover, Eric Johnston, then President Eisenhower's personal ambassador to the Middle East, was at that time in contact with Nasser. For the first time Mr. Johnston was getting some encouragement from Cairo in respect to his plan for equitable distribution of Jordan River waters between Arabs and Israelis. Most surprising of all to American diplomats was the fact that the United States Embassy, like Nasser, had heard of the forthcoming Allen visit via the Associated Press. There had been no message through official channels to the Embassy.

Although Mr. Allen enjoyed great popularity among his colleagues at the Department of State, it seemed to American diplomats on the scene in Cairo that his mission threatened to upset the delicate negotiations then going on between Mr. Roosevelt and Mr. Nasser. When the Embassy learned of Mr. Allen's impending arrival, these negotiations came to a standstill. It was possible for Roosevelt to go through the motions of carrying on discussions with Nasser, and it was possible for Eric Johnston to continue talking about the Jordan River plan. But both men considered their hands had been tied by the unknown quantity of what Mr. Allen intended to say.

When Mr. Allen actually arrived in Cairo, he was met by an imposing array of the United States government's best negotiating talent—Kermit Roosevelt, Eric Johnston, and Henry Byroade—all of whom advised him vigorously that an ultimatum was the last thing the situation needed. Following this explanation by the men on the scene, Mr. Allen agreed not to deliver his message. As a result, Allen's meeting with Nasser reportedly was a courteous but anticlimactic review of the current situation.

The fact of his coming at so critical a moment, however, particularly since it had been heralded by a news report saying he was carrying an ultimatum, effectively ended the negotiating efforts between Mr. Roosevelt and Mr. Nasser. The arms acceptance speech which the Egyptian leader finally delivered was not a prelude to possible reduction of tensions with Israel. Some American observers believe that had the State Department understood Nasser's dilemma and acted accordingly, the result would have been the saving of at least some of the American position in Egypt. As it was, the attitude of the United States implied by Mr. Allen's visit destroyed this possibility.

The great watershed had been crossed. Through the arms deal Russia was about to enter the Middle East on a wide front. The best the American Embassy could do was to sit quietly and await developments, although Ambassador Byroade made a few routine efforts to appeal to Nasser not to go too far too fast with his new friends. Mr. Byroade also urged the Egyptian leader to be on constant lookout for Soviet attempts to use their new prestige in Egypt for their own ends.

But clearly American-Egyptian relations had entered a new phase. In the eyes of Secretary Dulles the Egyptian leader had become a villain, the man who had introduced the Soviets to the Middle East, thereby undercutting Dulles' efforts to keep them out. The ensuing tension caused Mr. Byroade and Mr. Nasser to drop their first name basis and revert to formality.

Within Egypt—indeed, throughout most of the Arab world—Nasser had become a great hero who had torn Egypt from the domination of the West. No single act in his career to that time had so boosted his prestige as his purchase of Communist arms.

The State Department now concentrated on making things as difficult for Nasser as possible. The U.S. government tried to deny Egypt access to spare parts for American machinery, and it held back lubricating oils which Cairo ordinarily bought from the United States. At one point the possibility was discussed of "starving" the Egyptian people into rising against Nasser by cutting off American wheat shipments. CARE lunches for school children were cut off.

Mr. Nasser himself discounted the effects of this campaign. Egypt's standard of living already was so low, Nasser contended, that the American economic boycott could not further depress it; and the Egyptian economy was not as shaky as the State Department supposed it to be. Furthermore, said Nasser, anything the United States denied him, he could get from the Soviets. Already the Egyptian people were blaming what new economic hardship there was on the United States, not on Nasser. Thus U.S. economic warfare was only driving Nasser closer to the Soviets and was insuring the Egyptian people's acceptance of this new alignment.

Crowning act in the U.S. economic boycott was withdrawal of the offer of American help to build the High Aswan Dam. This withdrawal was seconded by the British, who also had pledged their assistance for the project. Internally, the United States foreign aid program was having trouble in Congress at this time. Opposition to American aid for the High Dam had developed in the Senate, particularly among cotton state senators who foresaw more cotton-producing acreage for Egypt, and among Western senators who had dam projects of their own to advance.

To some extent this internal factor weighed in Mr. Dulles' dramatic announcement July 19, 1956, that the U.S. would not help Egypt build the giant dam. Cairo had failed to reach agreement with the Sudan and other riparian states on division of the Nile waters, and the Egyptian economy appeared less able to sustain the huge project "than at the time the offer was made." Tone of the withdrawal was sharp and its implication was that the arms deal with the Soviets had made the Egyptian economy financially unsound.

The West now expected that Russia would fail to come

through on its vague offers of help for the dam and that Mr. Nasser would be left high and dry, in a chastened mood. In part the West was correct. Russia secretly offered to contribute to the dam—but only if President Nasser restored free political party life in Egypt. To Mr. Nasser this was aid with strings attached and he turned it down. Publicly Soviet Foreign Minister Dimitri Shepilov said the U.S.S.R. was not considering aid to Egypt for the dam, a project less "acute" than the United States thought it was.

Nasser's bombshell reaction to the loss of aid took the West by surprise. Thoroughly angry, the Egyptian President studied reports which already had been drawn up, forecasting the Egyptian government's task in taking over the Suez Canal Company at the time its concession expired in 1968. Then, with a few of his closest subordinates, Nasser held an emergency meeting to estimate what world reaction would be if he nationalized the Suez Canal Company immediately.

Their consensus was that a great international flurry would ensue for about forty-eight hours, but that by the time Britain and France had decided on drastic action, world opinion no longer would support them. Armed with this estimate, President Nasser told the Egyptian people on July 26, 1956, in a speech filled with rage against the West, that the canal company had been nationalized.

His hero status rose to new heights in the Middle East. Frenzied Egyptian crowds greeted his return to Cairo from Alexandria, where he had delivered the speech. Throughout the Arab world he was increasingly compared with Saladin, the legendary Arab general who had wrested Jerusalem from the Crusaders in the 12th century.

The United States, in common with other Western powers, was convinced the Egyptians could not run the canal. To add weight to this conviction the State Department urged American pilots to resign. American ship owners were advised that transit through the canal would be unsafe. At midnight on September 14, British and French pilots were ordered off their jobs by the old Suez Canal Company.

Under the direction of Col. Mahmoud Yunes, Egypt's nationalized Suez Canal Authority was left with 26 trained pilots and 30 trainees in place of the 250 pilots normally required.[1] Nonetheless traffic continued to move through the canal without hitch. The very night British and French pilots walked off their ships, fifteen Soviet pilots arrived at Colonel Yunes' office. Soon these "volunteers" were joined by actual volunteers from the United States, India, Iran, Greece, and elsewhere. From then on the canal was managed as efficiently by the Egyptians as it had been by the highly professional Suez Canal Company.

Some changes were taking place in State Department thinking about Nasser. The West's economic blockade had strengthened, rather than weakened, him in the eyes of his people, and was having the result which Nasser himself had predicted—it was driving him toward the Soviets. Moreover, United States policy now was preoccupied with preventing Britain and France from going to war against Egypt, thereby threatening Western oil installations in the Middle East and possibly world peace.

To sidetrack Britain and France from desperate action the United States took part in committees to devise some form of international control over the canal. Chief outcome of the staff work was the fifteen-nation Suez Canal Users'

[1] Wilton Wynn, *Nasser of Egypt: The Search for Dignity* (Cambridge, Massachusetts: Arlington Books, Inc., 1959), p. 177.

Association, which accomplished little beyond setting up an operating budget and choosing an administrator.

By mid-October it was plain the British and French were building up a military striking force on the island of Cyprus. Secretary Dulles warned that the United States opposed aggression in the Middle East and would aid its victims. When the blow actually fell—a three-pronged Israeli-French-British attack against Egypt at the end of October—the United States took the lead in forcing an end to hostilities and the withdrawal of foreign troops from Egypt.

To some extent this support mitigated the effects of the earlier U.S. economic blockade. All along, President Nasser had maintained the belief that there was friendship toward him in segments of the United States government, but he remained convinced that Mr. Dulles was out to destroy him. To American friends who visited him in 1957 Nasser expressed the view that were it not for Secretary Dulles' personal animosity toward him, it still would be possible to establish a mutually satisfactory modus vivendi between the United States and Egypt, despite differences over the question of Israel.

Nasser once expressed the view that "Secretary Dulles is the one individual most responsible for causing conditions in the Middle East which the Soviets best know how to exploit." Nasser suggested that Dulles was doing this at tremendous cost to American interests only for the purpose of helping Israel. On this subject President Nasser appeared to be beyond the reach of reason. At one point he instructed his Embassy in Washington to investigate the "extent of collusion between Secretary Dulles and the Zionists," since Nasser interpreted many of the Secretary's actions as apparent willingness to back Israel regardless of the cost to American interests.

The chief difference between Egypt and the U.S., Nasser once told a foreign visitor, was that the United States wanted the Arabs to remain split in order to prevent their domination by Nasser, while Cairo was determined to unite the Arabs so they could "be strong both in the face of the West and in the face of the Soviets." Nasser was certain he would win in the long run. But he feared short-term successes by Washington "because the United States has money to spend and the Arab countries have corrupt leaders who will accept it."

Nasser was convinced that American intelligence agents were stirring up anti-Nasser opposition throughout the Middle East. Specifically, he accused American agents of being behind King Hussein's ouster of pro-Nasser elements from the Jordan government and army in April, 1957; of stimulating the hostility of Lebanese Christians toward Nasser; and of plotting the overthrow of the increasingly pro-Soviet Syrian government.

Strangely, these suspicions appeared not to erase the modicum of friendship which he continued to feel toward the United States. Nor did his suspicions disturb his relations with individual American friends, some of whom he thought were directly involved in anti-Egyptian intrigues. With respect to alleged American intrigues in Syria, Mr. Nasser appeared to consider them understandable efforts to prevent Syria being taken over by the Communists. He objected to these alleged activities only because he felt they would fail and thrust the Syrians closer to the Soviets.

During this 1957 period the State Department adopted Ambassador Hare's policy of "attentive inactivity" toward Cairo. (Mr. Hare had become U.S. Ambassador to Egypt on August 14, 1956.) The American economic boycott of Cairo had been stopped and there was an effort to convince the Egyptians of United States concern and interest, without doing much specific about it. Meanwhile, America continued its warm support of Arab leaders who were Nasser's enemies. For his part Mr. Nasser had narrowed his suspicions of the United States government down to Secretary of State Dulles.

The merger of Egypt and Syria in the United Arab Republic on Feb. 1, 1958, had no marked effect on American-Egyptian relations, beyond the fact that Washington welcomed it as a move to frustrate a Communist coup of Syria. Essentially the merger had been just that.

At the end of 1957 some leading non-Communist Syrians, including President Kuwatly, who had been re-elected on August 18, 1955, Prime Minister Sabri el-Assali, Foreign Minister Salah Bitar, and Baath Party leader Akram Hourani, had given up their tentative plans to crack down on Syrian Communists. Feeling themselves too weak to make the effort alone, they saw Syria's only solution in a merger with Egypt.

At first Nasser had been cool to the idea, and had stressed the differences between the two countries—Syria had political parties, Egypt had none; the Syrian Army was involved in politics, the Egyptian Army was not. But Salah Bitar, who had led a Syrian delegation to Cairo in January, 1958, said that Mr. Nasser had two alternatives—either help to solve Syria's problems through union, or watch Syria march into the Soviet camp, with Egypt possibly following.

Despite his own misgivings, President Nasser agreed to the merger. With great fanfare the birth of the United Arab Republic was announced on February 1, the first step, it was declared, toward federation of all Arab states.

On February 25 the United States formally recognized the new merger and took steps to downgrade its Damascus Embassy to a consulate general. On February 26 Mr. Dulles said the merger of Egypt and Syria gave reason to hope the two countries were more determined to avoid falling under the control of international communism.

By now Washington and Cairo were watching each other warily to see if their relations might not be improved by concrete acts of cooperation. In part President Nasser was led to this by his aroused suspicions of the Soviets. In talks with Americans Nasser stressed the "common problem" facing the U.S. and U.A.R. in the Middle East—to prevent a Soviet conquest. Surely the United States must realize, Mr. Nasser's reasoning ran, that it could not fight Soviet influence on one hand and the influence of Nasser on the other. To fight them both would merely drive communism and Arab nationalism together.

By no means had all suspicion vanished. On March 5 Lt. Col. Abdel Hamid Serraj, the U.A.R.'s new Minister of Interior for Syria, accused King Saud of Saudi Arabia of plotting to assassinate President Nasser and thwart the Egyptian-Syrian union. The United States was involved in the plot, Serraj alleged. On March 24 Saudi Crown Prince Feisal took over real power from his brother, the King, in an effort to restore internal confidence in the Saudi dynasty. As a consequence the plot story subsided and died, without having affected the tentative moves Washington and Cairo were making in each other's direction.

By the spring of 1958 Washington and Cairo had turned nearly full circle in their attitude toward each other. The United States had learned that, willy-nilly, it must deal with President Nasser on his own terms or not at all, and that to cooperate with him might enhance American interests elsewhere in the Middle East. Mr. Nasser, thoroughly alarmed by his experience with the Soviets, had returned to the belief that the United States might be willing to help him without infringing his independence. Despite the scars acquired over the past few years, both sides appeared ready to open a new phase in American-Egyptian relations.

CHAPTER 4

# The Long Road Back

Starting early in 1958, American relations with the U.A.R. suddenly began to improve. Chiefly responsible for the concrete steps taken on the American side was Ambassador Raymond Hare, who had succeeded Mr. Byroade in Cairo. To Mr. Hare conditions now seemed ripe to quicken a bit the recent American policy of "attentive inactivity." Nonetheless, the long road back toward good relations between the United States and Egypt had to be traveled quietly, unspectacularly, and with no set schedule of achievement in mind. To lay down a fixed program of steps to be accomplished would only arouse Egyptian suspicions that a kind of "pact mentality" still dominated State Department thinking.

Instead, the American Embassy in Cairo waited until President Nasser's disenchantment with the Communists made him receptive to some gesture by the United States. Then it was Mr. Hare's task to persuade his superiors at home that such a gesture would not be used by Mr. Nasser to play one side against the other, as Washington felt its aid had been used since the Soviet arms deal of 1955.

Thus the United States and the U.A.R. quietly began to grope toward a better understanding of each other and with each other. In the early stages of *rapprochement* neither side fully trusted the other and both sides were aware that undue publicity might destroy what cautious progress was being made. Mr. Nasser in particular had to avoid the charge that he was blundering into the arms of American imperialism in his effort to escape the Communists.

In August, 1958, a first tentative step was taken when the United States released $400,000 worth of road-building and other equipment which originally had been earmarked for Egypt but which had been held in the U.S. since November, 1956. The following month the United States government allowed CARE to resume its school lunch feeding program for more than one million Egyptian children. Though the handling of the food was done by CARE, the food supplies themselves—mostly dried milk and cheese —were supplied by the United States government. Also in September Washington released Egypt's frozen sterling balances in the States, amounting to about $21,000,000.

On December 22, 1958, the Suez Canal Authority leased the giant U.S. Army hopper dredge "Essayon," to be used primarily for deepening the Bitter Lakes in the Suez Canal and improving the harbor of Port Said. Used twenty-four hours a day, seven days a week over the rental period of six months, the "Essayon" was leased to the Egyptians at a price $1,600 per day less than an American firm would have had to pay.

In December, 1958, the United States agreed to sell Egypt $25,000,000 worth of wheat for Egyptian pounds, under the Agricultural Trade and Development and Assistance Act of 1954 (popularly called Public Law 480). This was the first of a series of agreements under which this kind of American aid to Cairo increased to more than $100,000,000 by the spring of 1960.

Enacted by Congress in July, 1954, Public Law 480 has three titles or sections, of which the most widely used is Title I. Under Title I, surplus commodities are sold to a country in return for its local currency. These local currency receipts then are put to work within the country concerned.

In Egypt, for example, some of the local currency earned has been loaned back to the U.A.R. government for development projects. Other funds are used to pay American Embassy and consular expenses within the U.A.R. Twenty-five per cent of the money earned can be loaned to American businessmen desiring to enter or expand their operations in the U.A.R. market. Some of the wheat sale funds were used to pay for an exchange of students and teachers when the Fulbright educational exchange program was renewed by Washington and Cairo on September 28, 1959. It was at this time that Cairo, quietly but urgently, was withdrawing a large number of its students from Communist-bloc schools and sending them to the West.

In March, 1959, Washington released $7,985,000 in old economic assistance funds to Egypt, frozen at the time of the Suez crisis. American Point Four aid to Cairo was resumed, initially for highway development and the training of civil aviation specialists. In April, 1959, American specialists returned to Cairo to help with the draining of Egyptian swamplands under the aegis of the Egyptian-American Rural Improvement Service (EARIS). So far under this program, two areas of land—one west of Alexandria near the Mediterranean Sea and the other at Fayum southwest of Cairo—are being drained, leached, and prepared to grow grain crops.

Other normalization steps include the loan of $5,000,000 by the Export-Import Bank to an Egyptian chemical factory; the completion of negotiations for a treaty avoiding double taxation for nationals of the two countries; and the hiring by Egypt of American firms to aid in Suez Canal improvements. These moves were capped in December, 1959, by the granting of a $56,500,000 World Bank loan for widening and deepening the Suez Canal. This loan was granted over the protest of sixty-six Congressmen, who urged the State Department to hold up the loan until President Nasser allowed Israeli shipping to use the canal.

The Egyptians also asked for and received the services of an American expert from the United States Geologic Survey to probe the water potentialities of a great trough-like depression in the Libyan Desert west of the Nile. Marked principally by the Kharga and Dakhla oases, this valley in ancient times had supported a population which cultivated an estimated 8,000,000 acres of land. In early Islamic days the main road from Egypt to the Sudan ran through the two oases.

Gradually, as the centuries wore on and the Nile River was brought under control, the people of the oases drifted eastward to the river valley, until today perhaps 45,000 persons are left at Kharga and Dakhla, eking out a bare living from subsistence farming and the raising of flocks. These people live isolated from the rest of Egypt. Only camel caravans connect the oases with each other and with the Nile Valley. Nothing remains to indicate that here, in ancient times, was a flourishing part of Egypt.

Nothing, that is, except the belief of the Egyptian government that a huge underground river of water flows from south to north beneath the Kharga and Dakhla depression, and that this water can be tapped to make the depression a productive home for hundreds of thousands of Egyptian fellahin, or peasants.

Eighteen water wells have been drilled to date, nine at each oasis, and each flows freely without pumping. At the request of the United Arab Republic, a hydrogeologic report on the depression was made by the Expanded Program of Technical Assistance of the United Nations. This report, dated June 13, 1959, found justification for Cairo's desire to develop the oases, though the report pointed out that a good deal of critical survey work still lay ahead.

It was to participate in this work that Cairo asked for the services of an American geologic expert. His main job was to determine, if possible, whether the underground water was a self-replenishing river which could be tapped without depletion. On the answer to this hangs the future of the New Valley, as the project has been dubbed by the Egyptians, for the discovery that the groundwater was not self-replenishing would destroy hopes that the depression could be made to absorb some of the Nile valley's surplus population.

When I asked President Nasser about Egypt's development plans in October, 1959, he spoke enthusiastically about the potentialities of the New Valley. To many Egyptians the project ranks in importance with the High Aswan Dam as a possible answer to the Nile's land-hungry millions.

By the summer of 1959 the trend toward better U.S.-U.A.R. relations was well established, but the renewal of American help had been confined to Egypt, southern region of the United Arab Republic. Then came the Iraqi revolu-

tion of July 14, 1958, with its implied threat to President
Nasser's hold over Syria, the still shaky northern region
of the U.A.R. Quietly the Egyptians asked that United
States aid be extended to cover Syria as well as Egypt.

Never had a Syrian government accepted a penny of
United States aid. Traditionally the most anti-Western of
major Arab lands, Syria had rejected Point Four, despite
the program's obvious benefit to the underdeveloped Syrian
economy. Suspicion of the West was deeply ingrained in
the thinking of the Army officers and young Socialists who
had controlled Syria at the time of its merger with Egypt.
A leading spokesman of anti-Westernism had been Colonel
Serraj, former intelligence chief of the Syrian Army and
now Minister of Interior for the northern region of the
U.A.R. For President Nasser to introduce American economic aid into Syria meant flying in the face of his most
powerful Syrian lieutenant.

But the step was taken. On November 12, 1959, Washington announced that the Development Loan Fund would
loan $700,000 to a private Syrian firm to build a woolen
mill outside Damascus. Two days later the United States
made public the sale of $9,600,000 worth of wheat and
barley to Syria under a Public Law 480 agreement. These
commodities would be paid for in Syrian pounds, 50 per
cent of which would be plowed back as aid for Syrian
regional development plans. Another 25 per cent of the
proceeds would be loaned to Syrian import-export firms—
very likely to help them buy Western rather than Communist goods—while the remaining 25 per cent would help
to meet local United States expenses, including the cost of
running the American consulates general in Damascus and
Aleppo.

At the same time it was disclosed that since December,

1958, the value of deliveries of American surplus farm products to Egypt had totaled $107,000,000. The disclosure of this figure, together with the announcement of American aid to Syria, illustrated President Nasser's growing willingness to acknowlege the extent of cooperation between Washington and Cairo.

American aid to Egypt now could be spoken of freely as a trend. The impressive list of projects mutually agreed upon could be totaled up and published in the press. Clearly Egypt had reached the stage of being a major recipient of United States aid.

Even today caution still keynotes mention of American aid in Syria. New projects involving United States help to Damascus are under discussion between Cairo and Washington, but they are carefully screened from public view until they can be signed and put into operation. Syria, in other words, is now groping toward better relations with the United States just as Egypt was during 1958. The significant thing is that American aid has penetrated Syria, and the agency of this penetration is President Nasser.

By late spring of 1960 relations between the United States and U.A.R. were on as reasonably solid a footing as could be expected, given the active distrust which had had to be overcome. Barring the unexpected—for example, an Egyptian move against Israel that would force an American protest—there was no reason the Cairo-Washington axis should not continue to strengthen. At least both sides realize it is to their mutual benefit to have it do so.

Elsewhere in the Middle East, the United States has special relations with a number of countries, several of whom are acutely dependent on American good will. One such state is Jordan, whose economy is subsidized by the United States. Jordan had its beginning in 1921, when the

British carved a new nation from the desert east of Palestine and gave it to a Hashemite prince named Abdullah. The reasons for creating this nation were political—to keep Abdullah from marching north against the French in Syria, and to forge another link in a chain of pro-British governments across the Middle East to India.

Economics played no part in the decision, and from the first Jordan was forced to rely upon foreign subsidy. Today Abdullah's throne is occupied by his grandson, King Hussein, whose problems are immensely complicated by the trebling of Jordan's population after the Palestine war of 1948. At that time King Abdullah had unilaterally annexed to Jordan those parts of eastern Palestine not occupied by Israel. Though this gave Jordan additional land, it also gave her so many new people that the country lost ground in its efforts to feed and support itself.

As a result King Hussein's barren little kingdom spends approximately eight times more for its imports each year than it earns from exports. The consequent budget deficit is in the order of $70,000,000 yearly, and Jordan needs this amount of pump priming if economic hardship is not to lead to political unrest, which will threaten the stability of the country.

The Palestinian newcomers to Jordan, deeply embittered by the loss of their homeland, became overwhelmingly pro-Nasser in sentiment when the Egyptian leader adopted the mantle of protector of the Arabs against Israel. At the same time the Palestinians' attitude hardened against King Hussein because of his stanch pro-Westernism. On March 14, 1957, pressure from this element of the population forced King Hussein to abrogate the Anglo-Jordanian treaty. British subsidy was withdrawn along with the British themselves. Egypt, Syria, and Saudi Arabia, already mentally dividing up the little country, offered a replacement subsidy of nearly $36,000,000 yearly in money and arms.

In the spring of 1957 King Hussein forestalled dismemberment of his kingdom by dismissing his pro-Egyptian government and exiling Nasserist officers of the Arab Legion, including its chief of staff, Maj. Gen. Ali Abu Nuwar. It was then the United States stepped in with a grant of $10,000,000 in special economic aid to Jordan. Subsequently that figure swelled to its present total of $70,000,000 a year in money, goods, and services.

There are certain difficulties inherent in the present American policy toward Jordan. In my own trips to Jordan I have found widespread conviction among Jordanians that sooner or later the "artificial" monarchy in Jordan must disappear and their nonviable little nation somehow must be merged with a larger Arab entity. The fact that the Jordanian royal family, as well as Israel, Britain, and some American officials are opposed to such a merger cannot obscure the fact that a great majority of Jordanian citizens appear convinced that the *status quo* is both temporary and undesirable.

These Jordanians share this conviction with Arab nationalists throughout the Middle East, particularly those who believe that the ultimate goal of Arab nationalism is the unity of Arab lands. The United States antagonizes Arab nationalist opinion through Washington's support of a regime opposed by the bulk of Arab opinion.

There are compelling reasons for giving all aid possible to a brave young king who must be constantly on guard against revolt, and who would be helpless to provide for his people if foreign aid were withdrawn. Nonetheless, American aid to King Hussein tends to isolate the United

States from the main body of Arab opinion, at a time when the United States is trying elsewhere to identify itself with Arab nationalist goals.

There is a parallel between American policy toward the regime of the late Nuri es-Said in Iraq and the policy toward Jordan today. Washington supported the pro-Western authoritarian Premier Nuri, despite his unpopularity with the Iraqi masses, in the hope that his allocation of Iraqi oil royalties to Iraq's development program would provide an example of peaceful evolution toward an improved standard of living for an Arab people. This hope was dashed when the Iraqi revolution led by General Kassem violently overthrew Nuri himself and also the Royal Hashemite Family of Iraq.

The same elements which led to the explosion in Iraq appear to be present in Jordan, with the additional handicap that Jordan does not possess an oil income with which to try to lift the living standards of its people. No one is more aware of this dilemma than American officials charged with administering United States aid to Jordan. In the absence of any practical alternative, however, they see no substitute to the present policy of trying to stave off troubles in Jordan through subsidy of the Jordanian economy.

Indirectly the United States is helped at present by President Nasser, who fears that chaos in Jordan might cause Israel to move its army eastward to the Jordan River. This in turn would force Mr. Nasser to try to drive the Israelis back, a task for which the U.A.R. leader does not consider his armies ready. In every way possible, therefore, Cairo is trying to influence its supporters in Jordan to accept the *status quo*, at least temporarily. In the meantime, while the debtor-creditor relationship between the Jor-

danian and United States governments could not be called
normal, it is at least warmly cooperative.

For different reasons King Saud's huge desert kingdom
of Saudi Arabia also enjoys a cooperative relationship with
the United States. The bulk of the kingdom's income
comes from oil and this oil is produced by a totally
American-owned company, the Arabian American Oil
Company (Aramco). Despite Soviet blandishments, King
Saud has remained firmly committed to his alliance with
the United States.

This attitude is reciprocated by Washington. In March,
1958, Secretary of State Dulles called Saudi Arabia an
anchor of United States policy in the Middle East. Apart
from oil, one reason for the importance Washington at-
taches to Saudi Arabia is King Saud's lease to the United
States Air Force of the Dhahran airfield in the eastern part
of the kingdom. This lease was most recently renewed on
Feb. 8, 1957, while King Saud was making a state visit
to the United States.

In part King Saud's friendship with the United States
derives from the monarch's utter rejection of Communist
influence in his country. But beyond this the royal family
realizes that social changes wrought by oil have bred unrest
aimed at the symbol of the throne, which has become
immensely rich since petroleum was discovered beneath the
desert sands.

The profligacy and lavish spending habits of King Saud,
plus the insolence displayed by some of the huge number
of his princely brothers has become a byword throughout
the world. In May, 1960, an American told me that he and
his wife booked into a luxury hotel in Beirut. During their
first night they were disturbed by the almost constant play-
ing of a radio at full volume in the room next door. Protests

to the manager were of no avail. When the performance was repeated the second night, the American got up in the early hours and demanded to see the manager. Obviously agitated, the Lebanese told the American he could do nothing. The man next door was a Saudi prince. When asked to lower his radio, the prince had retorted that he would buy the hotel before he would do so.

The Saudi royal family has fallen into great disrepute among the Arabs. To no one is this more disturbing than to the Saudi people themselves, who see the greater part of their country's income from oil used to maintain an incredible number of princes. By the spring of 1958 antiroyal and pro-Nasser sentiment, sparked by the lavish and selfish spending habits of the royal family, had reached such a pitch that Crown Prince Feisal, dour younger brother of the King, took over control of the country in a bloodless palace coup, though Saud was permitted to keep the throne.

The aim of Prince Feisal was to restore a semblance of order to the kingdom's finances, wipe out the Saudi government's huge debt to Saudi merchants and foreign banks, and deflate the popular image of Nasser by substituting the image of a more responsible Saudi royalty in its place. To a great extent Crown Prince Feisal appears to have succeeded, though there is no reason to doubt that Nasser's attraction for many Saudis still exists.

Despite their private differences over the running of the country, King Saud and Prince Feisal are united in their desire to perpetuate the Saudi dynasty. Both men realize that should trouble between the Saudis and the Arabian American Oil Company lead to a loss of income, the kingdom would lose the prosperity which keeps unrest at bay. Thus friendship with the United States, whose nationals produce the oil, is a major plank of the foreign policy of King Saud and his brother.

America's relations with Lebanon gained a special status as a result of the Lebanese rebellion of 1958. To understand this, one must first comprehend the delicate knife-edge of Christian-Moslem relations on which Lebanon perennially balances. Always at the back of Christian Lebanese thinking is the fear that Lebanon's Moslems one day will demand that Lebanon reunite with Syria, to which Lebanon belonged before it was artificially carved out of the hinterland by the French after World War I.

The French purpose in creating Lebanon was to set up a state controlled by Mount Lebanon's Maronite Roman Catholics—and, incidentally, to attempt to perpetuate French influence in the Levant through this Christian minority. To make Lebanon economically viable the French were forced to slice predominantly Moslem coastal districts out of Syria and add them to Mount Lebanon. The result was a small country whose population, according to the French-controlled census of 1932, was fifty-five per cent Christian, forty-five per cent Moslem. An intricate system of government was established whereby each Lebanese sect was represented in the Cabinet, Parliament, and government secretariat. Thus, by tradition—so far never broken—the President of Lebanon is a Maronite; the Prime Minister a Sunni Moslem; Speaker of the House a Shiite Moslem, and so on.

This system worked fairly well even after the French evacuated Lebanon in 1945 and the country became an independent republic, until the Moslems of Lebanon became convinced they now were a majority in the nation. This, they held, had resulted from the higher Moslem birth rate and from Christian emigration to the Americas. To the

Moslem's plea for a new census and for consequent re-organization of the government should the census prove their point, the dominant Christians turned a deaf ear.

This situation reached the explosion point early in 1958. Rumors swept the country that President Chamoun would seek a second six years in office after his term ended on September 23, 1958. On March 27 eighty-two Lebanese leaders issued a manifesto warning Chamoun against seeking a second term. Despite this warning, a petition was launched calling for a special session of Parliament to amend the Lebanese Constitution to permit Mr. Chamoun to run. Such amendment would have required a two-thirds majority vote in Parliament. President Chamoun himself made no statement one way or the other on this question. Actually, the United States, British, and French governments, regarding Chamoun as a kind of counterweight to Nasser and therefore to be encouraged, had agreed among themselves that Mr. Chamoun should run again, and had so informed him.

The sense of crisis deepened. Opposition to Chamoun was strong among Lebanese Moslems, not only for internal political reasons, but because Mr. Chamoun was at logger-heads with President Nasser, for whom many Lebanese Moslems had warm regard. For his part, Mr. Chamoun was convinced that Cairo was trying to subvert Lebanon into joining the United Arab Republic. Backed generally by Christian Lebanese, President Chamoun was determined to keep his country independent.

During this period Chamoun informed President Nasser that Nasser might not realize to what an extent his name had become synonymous with terrorism in Lebanon. Nasser's agents, Chamoun contended, were sending back to Cairo falsely encouraging reports of the alleged readiness of Lebanon to join the U.A.R. Nasser was urged by Chamoun to send a trusted observer to Lebanon to study the situation. Full freedom would be given to the observer to investigate everywhere in the country.

In return Mr. Nasser made known to Chamoun Cairo's concern that Lebanon was being used as a base for fifth-column activities against the U.A.R. To Mr. Chamoun this was incomprehensible, since to him the evidence seemed overwhelmingly the other way around.

At this time President Chamoun said to one foreigner in effect: "There is abundant proof that the Egyptian Embassy is an umbrella for espionage activities of all kinds. I don't mind their spying so much as I mind their giving false information to Cairo. These spies do irreparable harm with their false information as well as with their provocations."

Lebanese Moslem leaders demanded a less openly pro-Western policy on the part of President Chamoun and a foreign policy friendly to President Nasser. Chamoun and his government refused. Incident lead to incident, and by mid-May a large segment of the Moslem population, as well as some Christians, were in various degrees of revolt against the government. Men, arms, and other supplies began streaming over the border from Syria to aid the Moslem rebels. On May 13 Mr. Chamoun's Foreign Minister, Charles Malik, accused the U.A.R. of having instigated and aided the rebellion.

President Chamoun was a firm friend of the United States. Unequivocally he had accepted the Eisenhower Doctrine in 1957, under which Washington had pledged itself to come to the aid of any Middle Eastern government threatened by international communism. Thus President Chamoun had ranged himself on the side of the United

States against the Soviet Union. Though Lebanon did not appear to be threatened by communism as such, Mr. Chamoun could hardly be abandoned by Washington in his hour of need. On May 14, therefore, the United States began an airlift of arms and police equipment to the Lebanese government and announced that the amphibious marine strength of the American Sixth Fleet in the Mediterranean was being doubled.

Within Lebanon the issues were becoming clear-cut. Rebel leaders demanded that President Chamoun resign immediately and said peace would not come until he did. Chamoun insisted he would serve out his term, though Prime Minister Sami es-Solh acknowledged on May 23 that his government would not seek a constitutional amendment to allow Mr. Chamoun to run again.

Meanwhile, the position of the American Embassy in Beirut was becoming more and more difficult. On the one hand, it had an obligation to Mr. Chamoun not only because he had been the only Arab leader to endorse the Eisenhower Doctrine, but also because Washington had indicated to President Chamoun its approval of his running again. On the other hand, the American Embassy, led by Ambassador Robert W. McClintock, realized that Mr. Chamoun's refusal to compromise with the opposition was damaging the United States in Arab eyes. Washington was being made to appear in support of a minority leader against the wishes of Lebanese public opinion. Mr. McClintock himself reportedly was of the opinion that no government could survive in Lebanon, or in any other Middle Eastern country, if it were discordantly out of tune with its environment.

By now the United Nations had become involved in the fray. On June 6 Foreign Minister Malik presented the

UN Security Council with Lebanon's accusations against the U.A.R. Four days later Secretary of State Dulles said there was "irrefutable evidence" of U.A.R. interference in Lebanon. On June 11 the Security Council voted to send observers to Lebanon. By the end of the month seven main UN observer posts had been established in the country.

At one point President Nasser suggested to the United States that Washington and Cairo try to work out a joint solution to the Lebanese crisis. The U.S. was backing the "ins," Nasser indicated, while the U.A.R. was backing the "outs." Why not get together, work out a compromise, and propose it to Lebanon? Though Mr. Nasser's suggestion was transmitted accurately by Ambassador Hare, the State Department interpreted it as an invitation for the United States to arbitrate between the U.A.R. and Lebanon. This interpretation was rejected by President Nasser as insulting.

Early in July the UN Observer Group in Lebanon reported back to the Security Council that there was no evidence of Syrian infiltration as charged by the Lebanese Government. Galo Plaza Lasso, Ecuadorean head of the UN observer group, followed this up by terming the Lebanese conflict a "civil war." On behalf of the Lebanese government, Dr. Malik took "strong exception" to the UN observers' report. Dr. Malik argued that the UN observer group had made no serious effort to get into rebel areas. A number of competent foreign observers on the scene supported the Foreign Minister in this belief, and insisted that evidence of Syrian infiltration and support to the rebels was overwhelmingly in evidence to anyone making an effort to find it.

On July 15, one day after the Iraqi rebellion, the United States landed marines in Lebanon. This was done, President

Eisenhower declared, to preserve the sovereignty and independence of Lebanon following an appeal by President Chamoun, who told his people he had asked for U.S. intervention only after exhausting all other resources to end the war.

Now the United States occupied the center of the stage. Lebanese Christians welcomed the American marines in the belief that the marines had been sent to crush the Moslem rebels and back up President Chamoun with an iron hand. Such was not the case. Having decided that only some kind of political compromise could preserve Lebanon's independent existence, the United States government dispatched its troops primarily to prevent the assassination of Mr. Chamoun and permit him to serve out his term. This much was owed him by Washington. Beyond that the Lebanese had to forge a political compact acceptable to both sides.

Under Secretary of State Robert Murphy joined with Ambassador McClintock in Beirut in knitting together the elements of compromise with Lebanese leaders. First sign of solution was the agreement of both sides on the candidature of Gen. Fuad Chehab, a Maronite Christian who was commander of the Lebanese Army, as new President of Lebanon. On July 31, by a vote of 48 to 7, the Chamber of Deputies elected General Chehab President of Lebanon, to succeed Mr. Chamoun on September 23.

Immediately upon assuming office in September President Chehab invited Rashid Karami, leader of the Moslem insurgents in the northern Lebanese city of Tripoli, to become Prime Minister. This invitation precipitated a brief counterrebellion by Christian elements in the country, who protested that the net effect of American intervention and the election of President Chehab had been to reward the rebels by giving them the premiership and a dominant voice in government. Terrorism had been rewarded, the Christians maintained. The new impasse was broken on October 15, when a four-man Cabinet was formed with two Christian and two Moslem ministers. Mr. Karami retained the premiership.

By the end of October the last of nearly 15,000 American military men had left Lebanon. Not a single Lebanese had been killed by an American bullet. Throughout the Middle East there was general recognition that this combination of American kid glove and mailed fist had been the decisive factor in achieving a settlement.

Only Lebanese Christians were bitterly disappointed by the American intervention. They pointed out that what the United States had brought into being was the very government which President Nasser had desired, since the U.A.R. leader earlier had expressed his approval of Chehab and Karami.

Many observers felt much more than this had been achieved. A Syrian threat to swallow at least the Moslem parts of Lebanon had been thwarted. Cairo had learned that Christian resistance to the dissolution of Lebanon was too strong to be broken without risking general war. And there was no indication that President Chehab and Prime Minister Karami, though more friendly toward Nasser than their predecessors, had any intention of surrendering their country to the U.A.R.

Supporters of American policy argued that had the United States backed Mr. Chamoun to the point of firing on Moslem Lebanese, the anger of Moslem Arabs throughout the Middle East would have made Christian Lebanese unsafe except when protected by foreign guns. The use of force would have caused the certain downfall of Lebanon, it was argued, as well as destruction of the American position in the Middle East.

Certainly Moslem-Christian wounds had been rubbed raw by the fighting. But both sides had learned that the other could not be defeated without massive outside help, and that foreign powers would not allow an international war to be fought over essentially local issues. Exhausted by their inconclusive struggle, embittered Moslem and Christian Lebanese at least were willing to give their sectarian method of government another try.

By a prompt grant of $10,000,000 to the new government, Washington made clear its continuing support of Lebanon. Since that time other types of American aid, including surplus agricultural products, have been made available to Beirut. The United States remains Lebanon's major source of foreign help, as well as its closest big-power ally.

Iran is another nation completely open about its alliance with the United States. On March 5, 1959, this alliance was formalized by the signing of a bilateral defense treaty between the two countries, pledging American assistance in the event of aggression against Iran. Shah Mohammed Reza Pahlevi's country also is a member of the Central Treaty Organization (CENTO), successor to the Baghdad Pact.

Iran is a huge country, as can be clearly seen by superimposing a map of Iran over a map of Europe drawn to the same scale. As this is done, imagine Iranian military units stationed as they are in their own country. When projected on a map of Europe, Iranian soldiers will seem to be stationed in London, Belgium, and central France, Geneva, Heidelberg, Berlin, Genoa, Warsaw, and Belgrade.

To defend this great sprawling territory, Iran has an Army of 160,000 men, an Air Force 4,000 men strong, and a Navy of 3,000. In addition, Iran has the services of United States military training missions, through which, since 1950, nearly half a billion dollars in equipment and training has been funneled to build up the Iranian armed forces.

Divided into three groups, these American missions have the broad functions of making Iranian armed forces capable of maintaining internal security, doing their share to defend Iran's 1,100-mile Soviet-Iranian border, and contributing to the defensive shield of CENTO. It is the second of these missions—defending the Soviet-Iranian frontier—which has done most to bring United States military aid to Iran, for Iran's Azerbaijan province is considered by experts to be the key, not only to the defense of Iran, but of the entire Middle East.

Through three main mountain passes in northwest Iran the Soviets would have the route of best access to the warm-water ports of the Persian Gulf, westward to the Suez Canal, and northward against Turkey's southern frontier. Fortunately these steep mountain passes are defensible, and—in the event of a direct Soviet attack—the Iranian Army is believed capable of a holding action until major Western forces can be brought into play. To guard against such an attack, and also to bolster the morale of Iran's Azerbaijanis, the main strength of the Iranian Army is concentrated in the northwest.

A second area of concern is the Zagros Mountain chain separating Iran and Iraq. Here again three main passes— Ruwandez, Sanandaj, and Kermanshah—would be the likely routes of any invader from the west, and here again strong concentrations of Iranian troops are placed.

Because of the American-Iranian bilateral defense treaty, a direct Soviet attack on Iran almost certainly would launch World War III by bringing the United States to Iran's defense. In view of this, it is thought highly unlikely that the Soviets would resort to direct attack in an attempt to conquer Iran. That is why Iran's relatively meager army of 160,000 men is considered sufficient for its main job of guarding strategic passes, maintaining internal security, and encouraging the belief among Iranians that their Army forms part of a strong shield against Soviet aggression.

Major concern of Iranian and American military planners today is the Soviet build-up in Iraq and Afghanistan, Iran's neighbors to west and east respectively. This build-up sets up the possibility of disguised Soviet intervention in Iran through Soviet-equipped Iraqi and Afghan armed forces, plus infiltration of Communist Kurds, Azerbaijanis, Uzbeks, and other minorities into Iran from Iraq, Afghanistan, and the Soviet Union itself.

This danger was sharply heightened after the July, 1958, revolution in Iraq, which not only introduced Soviet economic, technical, and military aid into Iraq but also caused Middle East Communists—including those of Iran—to regroup in Iraqi territory to coordinate new expansion policies.

In an interview with me in Teheran early in 1960, the Shah himself expressed concern over the Communist build-up in these neighboring states. "Afghanistan," the ruler said, "has three air bases built by the Soviets and three smaller ones being built by them. She has IL-28 jet bombers and MIG-17 jet fighters. Iraq has six air bases, also IL-28's and MIG-17's. Iran has one air base and only F-84 fighters."

I asked if the F-84's were not in process of replacement and he answered almost with scorn:

"Yes, but by what? F-86's, not a match for the MIGs."

The apparent answer to this—though I was not in a position to make it to a sensitive King—was that Iran's supply of trained pilots was small, and that the washout rate in training was high. The numbers and types of aircraft granted Iran by the United States are considered by experts to be up to the present rate of useful absorption by the Iranian Air Force. In addition, two new military air fields now are under construction in Iran.

Following the Iraqi revolution, the United States stepped up its military assistance program in Iran through a plan called "Counterbalance," which strengthened Iran's already established defense pattern—namely, a concentration of strength in the strategic northwest Azerbaijan province; a secondary grouping along the Zagros Mountain passes between Iran and Iraq; a third defensive line in northeastern Iran, with reserve units in the southern part of the country.

By spring of 1960 four key Iranian divisions in the Azerbaijan area had been built up to 85 per cent of their planned equipment and manpower strength. Further expansion awaited only garrison space. Modern infantry, artillery, and armored training centers had been established. Twenty-two scattered replacement training depots had been reorganized into seven tightly centralized and coordinated centers.

Already, American experts believe, Iran's armed forces would be able to handle any aggression by Iraqis or Afghans, or even by both, so long as Soviet personnel were not operating in these armies in disguise. Thus Iran, though not possessing aircraft as modern as its neighbors' planes, is considered fairly invulnerable against Iraqi or Afghan attack. Beyond this Teheran must rely on its bilateral defense treaty with the United States to give Iran real protection against any direct Soviet attack from the north. In the meantime, Iran's Army and gendarmerie forces are being trained to handle the threat of infiltration by Communist guerrillas, who strive to stir up opposition to Iran's royal regime.

All this effort would be of little avail, were Shah Mohammed Reza Pahlevi's throne to be toppled by political unrest. But the Shah's hold over the great mass of Iranian peasants is considered secure, partly because of the ruler's distribution of his personally owned Crown lands to landless farmers. The Army also is considered loyal to the Shah. Indeed, internal rivalries among Army officers often turn on the point of which group is more loyal to the King.

It is only among the urban middle class, professional people, and students that resentment of the graft and corruption in government and frustration at the lack of real political freedom is in danger of being turned against the Shah. Even this disaffection is somewhat mitigated by the current economic prosperity—made possible largely by American financial and economic aid—from which the middle class primarily benefits. Meanwhile, the United States is quietly encouraging the Shah to permit wider political activity, as a safety valve for pent-up frustrations.

Iran is in striking contrast to the Arabs in its friendship with Israel. Because Iran is a Moslem land, it keeps this friendship quiet. But evidence of cooperation between the two countries is readily available. Despite Iranian denials, Persian oil is sold to Israel and is the main source of supply for the Israeli pipeline running northward from the port of Elath on the Gulf of Aqaba.

El Al, the Israeli airline, runs regularly scheduled but unadvertised flights from Tel Aviv to Teheran, flying up the Mediterranean and across Turkey to avoid crossing Arab territory. Israel has a tiny but nonetheless operative "Point Four" technical assistance mission in Iran. Finally, the Iranians lean heavily on the Israeli intelligence service, which may account in part for Iran's suspicions of the Arabs.

Turkey dwarfs even Iran in the amount of United States military aid it has received. Figures disclosed by the Pentagon in February, 1960, showed that Turkey had received $1,717,231,000 in military assistance in the decade 1950-59. This made Turkey the fourth largest recipient of this kind of help under the Mutual Security Program, outranked only by France, Formosa, and Italy.

This aid testifies to Turkey's position as the strong eastern anchor of the North Atlantic Treaty Organization. Ankara, the Turkish capital, also is headquarters of the Central Treaty Organization. Finally, Turkey has a bilateral defense treaty with the United States, signed on March 5, 1959, the same day as Iran's similar treaty with America.

From the military point of view, this American investment has been a distinct success. Turkey's armed forces of approximately half a million well-trained and well-equipped soldiers form an invaluable bulwark between the Soviet Union and the Middle East. Ingrained in the tough Turkish character is a dislike and suspicion of the Russians going back for centuries.

Turkey has also received more than one billion dollars worth of American economic aid since President Truman announced a support program for that nation in 1947. Together the United States and Turkey have striven to broaden the Turkish economy by creating industry to supplement the country's agricultural base. To some extent this program has succeeded. Nonetheless, Turkey's adverse balance of trade continues to drain away the nation's foreign currency reserves.

In one sense American relations with Turkey were left undisturbed by the successful Turkish Army *coup d'état* which overthrew the government of Premier Adnan Menderes on May 27, 1960. That is, Turkish Army leaders are fully as pro-American and anti-Soviet as the civilian politicians whom they replaced. Gen. Cemal Gursel, leader of the Army junta which overthrew Menderes, assured American officials after the coup that foreign policy had played no part in the Army's action. Of this there is little doubt, though there is considerable doubt that the Army will be able to accomplish its professed goal of returning quickly to barracks and restoring the Turkish government to civilians.

For some time prior to the coup the Democratic party government led by Mr. Menderes had been throttling press freedoms, hobbling the opposition Republican People's party, and showing every intention of changing Turkey's two-party system to one-party rule under the Democrats. From the Turkish Army's point of view the final straw came when Mr. Menderes ordered the traditionally non-political Army to prevent opposition political meetings and to break up student crowds demonstrating against Mr. Menderes.

To halt this darkening trend the Turkish Army—or, rather, a 50-officer junta called the National Unity Committee—deposed the Turkish government on May 27. Arrested were President Celal Bayar, Premier Menderes, his entire cabinet, and all 404 Democratic Party deputies in the Grand National Assembly. The Turkish Constitution was scrapped and a committee of distinguished lawyers and judges was appointed to draw up a new one. Upon completion of the new Constitution, the National Unity Committee declared, a new Parliament would be elected, and the Army would withdraw in its favor. In the meantime, the National Unity Committee would wield total power in Turkey, and the "provisional" Cabinet headed by General Gursel would be responsible to it. Gursel himself adopted the title of chief of state, premier, and chairman of the National Unity Committee.

So far there is little reason to doubt the sincerity of the officers holding this unaccustomed power. Indeed, twelve members of the original 50-member junta were dropped from the National Unity Committee for refusing to take an oath that would have forbidden them to play any active political role in Turkey once a new Parliament was chosen. The remaining 38 members of the committee, led by General Gursel, did take the oath and are bound by their word to go back to being mere soldiers again.

Before they can do so, however, Turkey must be provided with a viable two-party political system. Otherwise there might be little to prevent the Republican People's party—the former opposition party and almost certain winners in Turkey's next elections—from gradually assuming the same totalitarian grip over the country as was exercised by ousted Premier Menderes and his Democratic party.

It should be recalled that in the late 1940's it was Mr. Menderes and Celal Bayar, as political "outs" and also voices of liberalism and democracy, who were charging President Ismet Inonu and his Republican People's party with the same stifling of freedom for which Mr. Menderes was overthrown. In 1950, public reaction against the Republicans brought Bayar and Menderes to power, the former as President and the latter as Premier. Since that time, the Democrats won two more elections—in 1954 and 1957—and Messrs. Menderes and Bayar gradually became as dictatorial in their control of Turkey as Mr. Inonu had been. On balance, there seems little to choose between Republicans and Democrats in their mutual tendency to rule in an iron-handed manner once they gain electoral control.

With only a paper Democratic party to contest the next elections, the Republicans would have it all their own way. Despite Mr. Inonu's call, immediately after General Gursel's *coup d'état,* for Republicans to control whatever vindictive feelings they might have, it must be assumed that thoughts of political revenge lurk in some Republican hearts. Yet to reconstitute a real Democratic party is difficult, since General Gursel arrested not only Bayar, Menderes, and the Democratic cabinet, but also all 404 Democratic deputies in the last Grand National Assembly. All these people, according to General Gursel, will be tried on charges of violating the Turkish Constitution, and only those who come off with clean hands will be allowed to contest the elections.

By arresting every Democratic deputy elected by Turkish voters the National Unity Committee has decimated the Democratic party leadership right down to the grass roots. Unless the trial of these people is handled with great tact and wisdom it may boomerang against General Gursel, since obviously many of these deputies will appear guilty only of obeying their party leaders.

Thoughtful Turks also are pondering the problem of what should be done with Mr. Menderes himself. He has done many good things for Turkey, and there seems reason to believe that widespread sympathy for him still may exist among the Turkish peasantry. Should Menderes be sentenced to prison, the reasoning runs, sympathy for him seems bound to grow. More and more his political excesses will be forgotten and his worthy accomplishments remembered.

This feeling could mushroom to the extent that the Democrats, should they win the elections in four years' time, might offer amnesty to Mr. Menderes and other party leaders. This could touch off a new Army revolution if officers felt the aims of their coup had been frustrated.

These are some of the reasons militating against an early return to barracks on the part of the National Unity Committee. In all likelihood it will be this committee, acting through a largely civilian cabinet, which will petition the United States for more aid with which to meet Turkey's economic and fiscal problems. When that petition comes, the United States, either alone or in concert with other powers, presumably will have to step in with new aid or risk losing its previous investment through deterioration of the Turkish economy.

It would take a volume to cover all aspects of Turkey's economic decline. Basically, however, the decline stemmed from inflationary policies initiated by the Menderes government, particularly from 1954 to 1958. These policies included short-term financing of foreign debts, heavy investment at home in industrial and agricultural development, and flooding the market with new money through huge extension of credit by Turkish banks, including the official Central Bank.

In 1956 the government tried to decree inflation out of existence by instituting a system of import licenses and price controls. By 1957 this system had become so complex that it was difficult for a Turkish businessman to complete a legal foreign-trade transaction. This effort at control was doomed to failure by the Turkish government's continued inflationary spending, including further rapid extension of credit and acceptance of new foreign debt commitments. As a result, the abundant money supply chased scarce goods in a flourishing and demoralizing black market. Concurrently, Turkish reserves of foreign exchange fell to zero and then into the red.

In August, 1958, at the urging of the United States, Turkey's European allies, and responsible Turkish leaders, Premier Menderes agreed to a drastic stabilization program, including devaluation of the Turkish pound from 2.8 to 9 to the dollar, application of rigid credit ceilings for Turkish banks, and removal of all direct economic controls. To support this effort, the United States and the Organization for European Economic Cooperation made available to Turkey an aid package worth more than $350,000,000. Furthermore, Turkey's foreign creditors, in an agreement signed in May, 1959, agreed to deferred payments on approximately $400,000,000 worth of Turkish debts.

For about eighteen months this stabilization program worked well. The black market disappeared, speculation in real estate stopped, and Turkish exports of fruits and vegetables, cement, sugar, and wool increased. At the beginning of 1960, however, Premier Menderes began to direct his efforts toward new elections scheduled for May. He went about the countryside promising new schools, village roads, and other improvements. These improvements were included in the Turkish budget for the fiscal year beginning March 1, 1960. By the end of April the government's vigorous spending had caused a cash budgetary deficit in the vicinity of $50,000,000.

On the eve of the *coup d'état*, the government was faced

with the alternative of breaching its own rigidly imposed credit ceilings, thus heralding a return to openly inflationary policies, or cutting down drastically on public spending. Premier Menderes was saved from this decision by General Gursel's coup. Gursel and the National Unity Committee have inherited the economic tangle bequeathed by the government they overthrew.

Another factor giving Turkish leaders pause is the rapid rise of Turkey's population, estimated at 3 per cent a year. Currently 27,000,000, Turkey's population is expected to double in less than thirty years and to reach 42,000,000 by 1975. This means Turkey must increase its productive capacity 3 per cent each year just to keep the standard of living where it is.

While these economic factors appear critical in the short term, the Turkish economy is basically strong in its agricultural potential as well as in forestry and mineral reserves. Also in General Gursel's favor is the fact that he has chosen trained Turkish economists to advise him. Finally, the general can count on the undoubted good will of the United States, which since 1947 has poured $3,000,000,000 into Turkey's economic and military development. Almost certainly sound fiscal policies by General Gursel's "provisional" government would be backed up by new United States aid to tide Turkey over difficult days ahead.

American relations with Israel are the subject of the next chapter. With the remaining countries of the Middle East and North Africa United States relations are not special in character. This does not mean they are unimportant; merely that there is little in American contacts with the Sudan, Libya, Tunisia, and Morocco to pull these relations out of the ordinary. Each of these nations inclines toward the West and accepts United States aid.

With Libya, the United States has an agreement to use the giant Wheelus Field airbase outside Tripoli. This airbase is capable of handling America's largest bombers. Use of the field was embodied in the United States-Libyan Agreement of 1954, currently up for revision in some details. In Morocco, President Eisenhower defused rising nationalist sentiment by agreeing to evacuate five United States Air Force bases on an accelerated time schedule.

This survey scotches the commonly held belief that the United States' many-faceted relations with the Middle East are strained. In part this belief arose from President Nasser's poor public image in the United States, and from the tendency of Arab nationalist leaders and press to lump the United States together with Britain and France as "imperialists." Almost always these public utterances are at variance with the working attitude of Arab governments toward the United States.

In fact, with Lebanon, Jordan, Saudi Arabia, Sudan, Libya, Tunisia, and Morocco, as well as with Israel, Turkey, and Iran, Washington maintains excellent individual relationships. Cooperation steadily is increasing between the United Arab Republic and the United States.

Only with Iraq are American relations poor, stemming from Premier Kassem's abrupt curtailment of all United States' military, economic, technical, and cultural programs immediately after the 1958 revolution. By the spring of 1960 the Iraqi attitude had softened to the point of negotiating a new cultural agreement with Washington, permitting the reopening of an American library in Baghdad and an exchange of teachers and students. This agreement became possible only after the Iraqi government returned to the United States Information Service its sequestered properties in Iraq.

CHAPTER 5

# The United States and Israel

No aspect of American Middle Eastern policy has produced as much emotion as United States relations with Israel. The reasons for this are two. First, creation of the Jewish state came shortly after the Nazi pogroms, when the West's conscience demanded that something be done for a people which had lost six million of its members. Thus criticism of Israel, and of the American role in its creation, tended to be branded "anti-Semitism," a charge repugnant to most Americans.

Second, United States support of Israel gravely damaged American interests elsewhere in the Middle East. The war which brought the Jewish state into being drove more than 700,000 Palestine Arabs from their homes. Whether this was the fault of the Arabs or of the Jews, or both, is disputed. Nonetheless, the American conscience has been given another problem with which to wrestle.

The tendency of some American politicians to use the Palestine dispute for their own political ends injected a note of cynicism and hypocrisy into the problem. There was no doubting the anguish of Jewish Americans at the plight of their brethren in Europe. Many American Jews ardently supported the creation of a Jewish homeland in Palestine. Many American politicians saw little reason to affront their Jewish constituents, particularly since the Arab side of the case was little known in the United States.

In the 1940's the world Zionist movement exerted increasing pressure on American leaders to support the Zionist position. This position had been set forth in the Biltmore Program drawn up by David Ben-Gurion, at that time head of the Jewish Agency's executive committee in Palestine and now Israeli Prime Minister. On May 11, 1942, the Biltmore Program was adopted by the American Zionist Organization in New York City. The program called for the creation of a Jewish state including all of Palestine, the formation of a Jewish army, scrapping of the British White Paper of 1939 (which had sharply curtailed Jewish immigration to Palestine), and unlimited Jewish immigration to the Holy Land, to be supervised by the Jewish Agency rather than by Britain.

In November, 1942, the Biltmore Program became the official policy of the World Zionist Organization. Implicit in the program was the decision of the Zionist movement to look toward the United States, rather than toward Britain, for effective external support of its aims. To this end the passage of pro-Zionist resolutions was secured from a number of state legislatures in the United States, as well as a statement from President Roosevelt favoring Zionist aspirations.

On August 31, 1945, President Truman appealed to British Prime Minister Clement Attlee for the immediate admission of one hundred thousand Jewish refugees to Palestine. (Since the end of World War I Britain had been the mandatory power in the Holy Land.) Britain suggested instead a joint Anglo-American Committee of Inquiry to study the problem. The pro-Zionist report of this committee was followed by the formation of a higher level Anglo-American Commission to study implementation of the committee's findings. When the higher commission turned in an inconclusive report, President Truman renewed his direct appeal to Mr. Attlee for the immediate admission of one hundred thousand Jews to Palestine.

There is little doubt that this second appeal was politically inspired. It came in the midst of an election campaign in which two Democrats, James M. Mead and Herbert Lehman, were facing an uphill battle for election respectively as Governor and Senator of New York State. Both men informed the White House that a pro-Zionist statement must be made immediately, since Thomas Dewey, Mr. Mead's opponent for Governor, was on the point of making one. All this was based on the assumption that the Zionists of New York would vote as a bloc for the candidate most favorable to their aims.[1]

The State Department was asked by the White House to draft a suitable statement. Meanwhile, New York called Washington again. President Truman must issue the statement, or Messrs. Mead and Lehman would issue it on their own, calling on the President to endorse it. This brought forth Mr. Truman's second appeal to Mr. Attlee for the admission of one hundred thousand Jews to Palestine. The date of this statement was October 4, 1946. Two days later Mr. Dewey, Republican candidate for Governor, declared that "not 100,000 but several hundreds of thousands" of

[1] See Kermit Roosevelt, "The Partition of Palestine: A Lesson in Pressure Politics," *Middle East Journal*, January, 1948.

Jews should be admitted to Palestine. Republicans as well as Democrats were responsive to Zionist votes.[2]

The Palestine dispute then entered the United Nations, Britain having called for a special session of the General Assembly to study it. An eleven-nation United Nations Special Committee on Palestine (UNSCOP) was formed. The committee traveled to Palestine and submitted a report to the General Assembly in the fall of 1947. A majority of UNSCOP favored the partition of Palestine into separate Arab and Jewish states, with an internationalized Jerusalem.

The stage was set for the acrimonious partition debate in the UN, with the United States strongly backing partition. Just as strenuously opposing partition were the Arab states and some other Asian powers. A straw vote, followed by a preliminary committee vote, showed that the necessary two-thirds majority could not be mustered for passage of the partition resolution.

At this point the Zionist organization chose as targets six nations which had opposed partition. These were Haiti, the Philippines, Liberia, Nationalist China, Greece, and Ethiopia. Intense pressure, including phone calls and telegrams from prominent Americans, was focused on the governments of these countries to induce them to change their votes.

An ex-Governor, a prominent Democrat with White House and other connections, personally telephoned Haiti urging that its delegation be instructed to change its vote. . . . A well-known economist also close to the White House, and acting in a liaison capacity for the Zionist organization, exerted his powers of persuasion upon the Liberian delegate.[3]

[2] New York Times, October 7, 1946, p. 5.
[3] Kermit Roosevelt, "The Partition of Palestine: A Lesson in Pressure Politics," Middle East Journal, January, 1948, p. 15.

Both Haiti and Liberia reversed themselves and voted for partition. So did the Philippines and Ethiopia, while China abstained from voting. Only Greece, of the six chosen "targets," held fast to its earlier convictions. The final result was the approval of partition by the UN on November 29, 1947.

Further evidence of the political nature of the U.S. government's stand on Palestine was furnished by Col. William A. Eddy, U.S. Minister to Saudi Arabia from 1944-1946. Writing after his retirement from service, Colonel Eddy described the recall to Washington of four American diplomats stationed in the Middle East—the U.S. Ministers in Egypt, Lebanon and Syria (a joint post), Saudi Arabia, and the Consul General to mandated Palestine.[4]

The time of the recall was October, 1946. Its purpose was to give President Truman the diplomats' views on the effects of American policy in Palestine. Spokesman of the group was George Wadsworth, who spoke for about twenty minutes. When he had finished, Colonel Eddy wrote, "Mr. Truman summed up his position with the utmost candor: 'I'm sorry, gentlemen, but I have to answer to hundreds of thousands who are anxious for the success of Zionism; I do not have hundreds of thousands of Arabs among my constituents.'"

Within Palestine the situation deteriorated quickly following the UN vote for partition. Bands of armed Arabs, determined to prevent partition of the country, entered Palestine to attack Jewish settlements. Casualties mounted on both sides. Foreseeing no solution and unwilling to maintain the burden longer, Britain ended its mandate over the country on May 14, 1948. The same day the Zionists

---

[4] William A. Eddy, *F.D.R. Meets Ibn Saud* (New York: American Friends of the Middle East, Inc., 1954), pp. 36-37.

proclaimed the establishment of the State of Israel. The first nation to recognize the new state was the United States, followed closely by the United Nations itself.

The next day Arab-Jewish war broke out. Armies from Egypt, Transjordan, Iraq, Syria and Lebanon invaded to drive out the Jews. Fought through the rest of the year, broken by two UN-engineered truces, the war ended finally on January 7, 1949. Israel had triumphed, gaining in excess of 30 per cent more territory than had been awarded to the Jewish state by the UN partition plan of 1947. During the fighting more than 700,000 Arabs had lost their homes.

The new boundaries, given "temporary" status by the armistice agreements which ended the shooting war, since have been frozen into permanence. The armistice has not yet been replaced by peace. Technically Israel and the Arabs still are at war. Before peace can come, the Arabs insist, Israel must surrender its 30 per cent additional territory and give Arab refugees the choice of returning to Palestine or receiving compensation for their loss. Israel refuses, on the grounds it won the extra land in a war in which it was the victim, not the aggressor, and that the Palestine Arabs fled at the urging of their own leaders. To the present day this stalemate has continued, broken by occasional outbursts of fighting, of which the most serious was the temporary Israeli conquest of Sinai in the fall of 1956.

From the standpoint of the Arabs the United States government, as a leading architect of Israel's creation, became an enemy in 1948. This aspect of the problem disturbed American diplomats in the Middle East. Unanimously these diplomats had agreed with Ambassador Wadsworth's estimate that U.S. support of Israel might cost the loss of the Middle East to Russia. To most American diplomats, it was not a case of being "pro-Arab" or "anti-Jewish." It was simply a fact that support of Israel inevitably entailed damage to wider American interests in the Middle East.

Discussing this question with other Americans at the time, one U.S. Ambassador to the Middle East declared: "If our government in Washington decides it wants to side with Israel, it is not our business as Ambassadors to Middle Eastern countries to object. But it is our job to point out very clearly what will be the costs involved."

The Ambassador went on to say that conceivably the U.S. government would decide to back Israel regardless of the cost. But it was wrong to pretend there would be no costs. To do so was to conceal from the American people facts they had a right to know. To inform the American people of expected Arab reaction to U.S. support of Israel and of the consequent damage to American interests in the Arab world, was not being "anti-Israel," the Ambassador asserted. It was making known to Americans all elements involved in the decision their government was taking. To conceal part of the equation was doing an injustice even to pro-Israeli Americans, since all Americans had a right to know that their government's policy threatened the possible loss of the Middle East to the Soviets.

In short, most Americans did not know—and perhaps still do not realize—that President Truman's decision to support the creation of Israel ran directly counter to the advice of American diplomats in the area. It was a case of White House fiat, based at least in part on internal American political considerations, versus the judgment of professional diplomats assigned to watch American interests overseas.

Obviously there was a humanitarian side to U.S. support of Israel. Very likely even hard-boiled American politicians with their eye on the ballot box were moved by the tragedy of European Jewry, and felt they were doing something to help this bereaved people. Certainly many American Jews who condoned or applied political pressure on the White House and other organs of government, were motivated primarily by a desperate urgency to help their coreligionists. At the time very few persons could have foreseen that the creation of Israel would rob more than 700,000 Arabs of their homes; that the Arabs of Palestine, in effect, would be made to pay for Nazi crimes.

In retrospect, American policy toward Palestine was a tangled skein, through which ran the conflicting threads of politics and altruism against a background of public ignorance of the issues involved.

Having done so much to bring Israel into being, the United States government was duty bound to nourish the new state through its formative years. The economic problems faced by Israel were enormous. Since it was created as a Jewish homeland, it had to prepare for a massive and continuing influx of Jewish immigrants. In 1948 and 1949 alone, Israel accepted 340,895 Jewish immigrants, or slightly more than half the total number of Jews living in Palestine on the day the state was born. Through most succeeding years to the present, except for the early 1950's, immigration continued to be heavy. In 1959, the last year for which figures are available, 23,045 Jews came to live in Israel.

These newcomers came to a country whose economy had to be developed almost from scratch, and which had pitifully few natural resources to permit a sound economy to be built. From the first, Israel suffered from an annual

trade deficit running between $250,000,000 and $300,000,-
000. This deficit was, of course, the excess of imports over
exports. In 1959 this trade gap stood at $303,000,000, which
would seem to indicate the economy had made no progress
at all.

Such was not the case. From 1948 through 1959, Israel
almost trebled its population, and the state's means of production—Israel's ability to feed, clothe, and provide her
people with consumer goods—had nearly to treble merely
to hold the trade gap at its accustomed level. The fact that
the trade deficit did not increase proved that Israel was
expanding its means of production at least in ratio to its
population growth.

Foreign aid was Israel's only hope of closing its budgetary
gap and permitting the nation to survive. This help came
from a variety of sources, including an initial $100,000,000
in sterling credits owned by Zionists in Palestine. A further
boost was given when the West German Government
agreed in 1952 to pay Israel $715,000,000, primarily in
goods, over a twelve-year period as partial repayment for
Nazi crimes against the Jews. This aid, scheduled to end in
1965, flows into Israel in yearly increments of $60,000,000
to $70,000,000.

By far the most substantial amount of help came from
the United States. Consistently from the state's inception
private American Jewry has contributed at least $60,000,000
a year through the United Jewish Appeal and another
$50,000,000 through purchase of State of Israel bonds. In
crisis years these private contributions have soared higher.
They form the bedrock of Jewish support on which the
Israeli economy depends.

The magnitude of official United States government aid
to Israel can best be seen by comparing it with official

American aid to Arab states over the same period of time. The following table compares total United States economic aid to Israel for each fiscal year with the totals to all Arab states combined. Arab states thus lumped together are Egypt, Iraq, Jordan, Lebanon, Saudi Arabia, and the Sudan. Figures are in millions of dollars, and include all varieties of economic aid—technical assistance, outright grants, Development Loan Fund loans, surplus farm products under the Public Law 480 program, and loans from the Export-Import Bank.

| | *U.S. Government Economic Aid to Israel since May, 1948* | *U.S. Government Economic Aid to Arab States since May, 1948* |
|---|---|---|
| Fiscal Year: | | |
| 1948 | none | 7.3 |
| 1949 | none | none |
| 1950 | 135.0 | none |
| 1951 | none | 4.8 |
| 1952 | 63.5 | 9.5 |
| 1953 | 73.7 | 20.1 |
| 1954 | 54.0 | 25.8 |
| 1955 | 54.6 | 56.2 |
| 1956 | 54.4 | 39.9 |
| 1957 | 37.5 | 37.68 |
| 1958 | 89.2 | 70.9 |
| 1959 | 52.4 | 114.5 |
| Grand total: | $614,300,000 | $386,480,000[5] |

[5] These figures supplied by the United States government exclude American donations to Palestine refugee relief, which have ranged between $20,000,000 and $30,000,000 a year from 1949 to the present.

The table shows that, except in 1948 and 1951, Israel received more aid from the United States government than did all Arab states combined until 1955. In that year the Arabs, taken together, received slightly more help than Israel. Not until 1959 were the Arabs given substantially more aid than the Jewish state received.

From now on, the Arabs are likely to receive considerably more American aid than Israel, not for political reasons but because the improved Israeli economy had been largely crossed off the list of foreign economies needing special assistance from the United States. The bulk of Israel's American aid in the near future is expected to be surplus farm products, sold under the Public Law 480 program. Currently United States aid to Jordan and to the United Arab Republic is greater than that scheduled for Israel.

The table also indicates that major American help to the Arabs began only when the Eisenhower administration came into office at the beginning of 1953. This reflected the new administration's desire to repair its relations with the Arabs by demonstrating impartiality between the two sides. By no means did President Eisenhower abandon Israel, as the recent totals of United States aid to the Jewish state disclose. American contributions to Israel's development program continued to be made. In a sense the United States was morally bound to do this, since each year an increasing percentage of Israel's population was made up of refugees who had played no part in the Arab-Jewish struggle of 1948.

Washington had no desire to cancel its friendship with Israel as an integral part of America's Middle Eastern policy. It did wish to demonstrate that the United States was determined to be fair to both sides, both in the distribution of aid and in the protection of Arabs and Israelis against military incursion by each other. This last was made clear in 1956 when the United States demanded that Israel, together with Britain and France, retreat from Egyptian territory after the Suez war.

In this crisis President Eisenhower had the power to shut off donations by American Jews to Israel by invoking the Trading with the Enemy Act of 1941 and the Export

Control Act of 1949. This was an ultimate weapon, to be used only if Israeli actions threatened the Middle Eastern *status quo* and possibly world peace. But the possibility that this weapon might be used influenced Israeli Premier Ben-Gurion to withdraw the last of his forces from Sinai in March, 1957. He told his people that economic sanctions would make it impossible for Israel to continue its mission of gathering in its exiles from the world.

It was no great trick for Washington to persuade the governments of Lebanon, Jordan, Saudi Arabia, the Sudan, and the former Iraqi regime to cooperate with the United States despite the latter's friendship with Israel. These Arab governments needed American help and were willing to accept it without making too much fuss about Israel. It was different with President Nasser until his own disillusionment with the Soviets and a friendlier State Department attitude toward him permitted the resumption of United States aid to Egypt. By the beginning of 1960 it seemed clear that Mr. Nasser also saw no absolute bar to American-Arab cooperation in Washington's relations with Israel. The totals of American aid accepted by the U.A.R. since 1958 have testified to this.

Meanwhile, within the Jewish state the Israeli people were making impressive strides toward the still-distant goal of self-sufficiency. In 1959 Israel had a particularly progressive year. Foreign currency reserves rose from $94,100,000 at the end of 1958 to an estimated $155,000,000 one year later. The exports of goods and services increased by 24 per cent, from $237,200,000 in 1958 to $294,700,000 in 1959. In real terms the increase amounted to 30 per cent, but a slight decline in prices pulled the money value of exports down. Imports rose slightly by 4.5 per cent in real value.

In 1959 prices rose only 1.8 per cent within Israel, indicating that the state had turned the corner in the battle against inflation. This compared with a steady price rise of from three to four per cent in previous years, and a total rise in the cost of living index of nearly 350 per cent since 1950. Coupled with price stability was a rise of about eight per cent in consumption of products per head of population.

The nation's deficit in balance of payments fell by $32,000,000 or 9.6 per cent from $335,000,000 to $303,-000,000 at the end of 1959. This would have been improved still further, according to David Horowitz, Governor of the Bank of Israel, had the state not invested in new ships during the year. If the ships had not been bought, the trade gap would have been no more than $180,000,000.

Foreign aid still is the indispensable means of closing the payments gap. In 1960, Mr. Horowitz said, Israel hoped for $60,000,000 to $70,000,000 in private gifts from world Jewry, primarily in the United States; $50,000,000 from the sale of State of Israel bonds; about $60,000,000 in U.S. government help, mostly surplus food products; private foreign capital investment totalling $30,000,000; $70,000,-000 in West German reparations, and an additional $60,-000,000 in German restitution payments to individual Israeli families.

Thus Israel's economic progress was relative. The best efforts of a dedicated and resourceful citizenry presumably could not wipe out the nation's trade gap in the foreseeable future. Barring the way to self-sufficiency was the need for huge capital investment to create productive capacity for a rapidly growing population. Though immigration in 1959 stood at the relatively low figure of 23,045, Israel's total population increased by 57,023 during the year. (On January 1, 1960, the nation's population stood at 2,088,685 persons, including 1,858,841 Jews and 229,844 non-Jews, most of whom were Arabs.) Nonetheless, in virtually every sector the Israeli economy had progressed in real terms in 1959, and from this Israelis could take satisfaction.

Looking at all this from the American viewpoint, it might seem that the goal of harmonious relations with both sides in the Middle East was being achieved. The facts were not quite so simple. Israel's progress was being made in the face of Arab hostility that was, if anything, growing. The Suez Canal remained barred to Israeli shipping, even to Israeli cargoes carried on non-Israeli ships. The best efforts of UN Secretary General Dag Hammarskjold had failed to budge President Nasser from his refusal to allow Israeli cargoes through the canal.

Despite this refusal, the World Bank had granted Cairo a $56,500,000 loan to widen and deepen the Suez Canal. American aid shipments to both regions of the U.A.R. were increasing. And the Soviets now had pledged themselves to build both stages of Egypt's High Aswan Dam. To Israel it appeared that President Nasser was getting everything his way, and that the United States might be slipping over to a pro-Arab rather than neutral stand.

Israel had laid particular stress on Mr. Hammarskjold's efforts to open the Suez Canal to Israeli cargoes. After the clearing of the canal, which had been blockaded during the Suez hostilities, Israeli cargoes on non-Israeli ships were quietly allowed through the waterway by Egypt. Israel claims that more than forty of its cargoes passed through in that way. In March, 1959, the U.A.R. Government began stopping even this kind of "invisible" Israeli commerce. The situation came to a head in May when the Danish freighter "Inge Toft," bound for the Far East with an Israeli cargo, was halted by the Egyptians at Port Said, northern terminus of the canal.

Western diplomats pointed out to President Nasser that a number of nations who were neither pro-Arab nor pro-Israel were nonetheless "pro-international law." They might take a dim view of Egypt's flouting of three documents guaranteeing freedom of passage through the historic waterway—the Constantinople Convention of 1888; a Security Council resolution of Sept. 1, 1951, urging Egypt to stop interfering in the canal; and Egypt's own declaration of April 24, 1957, promising to respect the Constantinople Convention and to allow free navigation through the canal. It was this last declaration which had allowed more than forty Israeli cargoes to transit the canal unhindered.

President Nasser finally agreed to the following concessions, worked out in separate talks with the Egyptians and Israelis by Secretary General Hammarskjold:

1. Israeli cargoes could pass through the Suez Canal if:
   a. There was no publication by Israel of their movement.
   b. They were carried in non-Israeli flag ships, though the vessels might be chartered by Israel.
2. It was also stipulated that cargoes leaving Israel must be F.O.B. (free on board), meaning that ownership had passed to the purchaser by the time the cargoes went through the canal.
3. Cargoes inbound for Israel must be carried C.I.F. (cost, freight, insurance), meaning the cargo still was owned by the nation exporting it to Israel.

Despite the awkwardness this entailed for Israel, her government agreed to give the formula a try. Mr. Hammarskjold since has denied that any formal undertaking was reached on the matter, though Israel insists she was given to understand that the formula would work. It did not. In December, 1959, Egypt stopped the Greek ship "Astypalea," bound for Djibouti, French Somaliland, with a cargo of Israeli cement. This was the first Israeli cargo aimed at the canal since the detention of the "Inge Toft" in May.

Mr. Hammarskjold's endeavors to find out what had gone wrong with the formula were futile. In the end both the "Inge Toft" and "Astypalea" were forced to unload their cargoes at Port Said and sail away empty. Israel was especially embittered by the fact that President Nasser won his World Bank loan three days after the "Astypalea" was stopped. There the matter rests, with no visible prospect that Israel can get her cargoes through the Suez Canal short of resorting to violence.

Also disturbing to Israel is the Arabs' continued insistence they will go to war rather than permit the Jewish state to divert the Jordan River to water the thirsty Negev in southern Israel, where many Israeli newcomers now are being settled. The problem would not have arisen had the Arabs accepted the so-called Johnston Plan for dividing Jordan waters between Arab states and Israel.

In four trips to the Middle East from 1953 to 1955, Eric Johnston, as President Eisenhower's special ambassador, worked out a scheme for sharing the Jordan River which would have given sixty per cent of Jordan's unused water to Lebanon, Syria, and Jordan, and forty per cent to Israel. Though technicians on both sides agreed the plan was fair and feasible, the Arab governments in 1955 "postponed" consideration of the plan. Since that time the Johnston Plan has hung fire.

At the end of 1959 a fuss arose from a statement by Israeli Finance Minister Levi Eshkol that diversion of the Jordan River had become a top-priority project to Israel. This statement sprang from Israeli concern that continued immigration and the farming of new lands were dangerously taxing Israel's water supply. To remedy this situation Israel was preparing a 108-inch concrete pipeline system to pump 10,600,000,000 cubic feet of water yearly from the Jordan River southward to the parched Negev.

This pipeline cannot be used until its final link with the Jordan River is completed. Originally this link was scheduled to be at B'not Yaakov Bridge on the Jordan River between Lake Huleh and the Sea of Galilee. This stretch lies in a demilitarized zone between Syria and Israel, and in 1953 Syria obtained a United Nations order halting Israeli work in the zone. Since that time, Israel has concentrated on completing the pipeline system within its own borders.

Now the Israeli Government has shifted its planned diversion point several miles southward to a place just north of the Sea of Galilee and wholly within Israel. This change of plans greatly complicates Israel's problem of lifting water from the Jordan River bed to a reservoir at Sahl Batouf, near Nazareth, whence the water is scheduled to enter the giant pipeline and flow south to the Negev. Sahl Batouf reservoir now is virtually complete, as is the 108-inch concrete pipeline running 75 miles from the reservoir to the Negev.

But the installations needed to lift the water uphill to Sahl Batouf remain to be built. It will be at least the middle of 1961 before Israel is able to link up the Jordan River with the reservoir, even if the Jewish state gets the outside financing it needs to complete the project. Twice during 1959 Israel applied for United States government aid for its Jordan diversion project and both times was turned down. Reportedly Israel was advised by the United States to seek private financing for its plans. Meanwhile, the Arabs insist they will fight to prevent diversion of the river even if it takes place wholly within Israel. Such diversion, the Arabs allege, would increase the salinity of the Jordan River below the Sea of Galilee, spoiling the river for irrigation in the kingdom of Jordan.

Thus an aura of frustration and uncertainty dogs two of Israel's cherished hopes—free passage through the Suez Canal and diversion of the Jordan to make the Negev hospitable. To the Israelis, their comparative economic progress is being achieved within a hostile net cast by the Arab states and being drawn tighter and tighter about them. Not only has the United Nations proven powerless to help them, but the United States appears to be aiding the Arab boycott, the Israelis charge. Under the terms of the anti-Israel boycott inaugurated by the Arab League, the Arab states refuse to buy Israeli goods and blacklist foreign firms and ships dealing with the Jewish state.

In January, 1960, it was revealed that the United States Navy was including a clause in its contracts with oil tankers giving the Navy the right to cancel the charter if the tanker were denied access to an Arab port because of previous traffic with Israel. Specifically, the U.S. Military Sea Transport Service (M.S.T.S.) was seeking to avoid repetition of an incident which occurred December 18, 1957, when the tanker "National Peace" was denied port facilities to pick up an oil cargo at Ras Tanura, Saudi Arabia. Under the name "S.S. Memory," the tanker previously had traded with Israel. When the Navy canceled the contract and chose another ship, owners of the "National Peace"— the Pan Cargo Shipping Corporation and National Shipping and Trading Corporation of New York—sued the Navy for breach of contract and $160,000 damages.

Following this incident, the Navy inserted options into its contracts authorizing the Navy to cancel, without cost to itself, the charter of any ship "in the event the vessel is prevented from loading or discharging in any port by the local authorities because of the vessel having previously traded with Israel."[6] Though the Navy denied the clause was intended to support any political boycott, in effect American ships which had traded with Israel were excluded from bidding on Navy contracts.

After inquiries by several Congressmen into the "Haifa clause," as the option became known in shipping circles, the Navy agreed on February 18, 1960, to eliminate the clause from future contracts. The Navy declared:

The clause was adopted with no intention to give support to any political boycott. It was deemed advantageous to both the Government and shipowners. However, M.S.T.S. can accomplish its mission without using the clause. Inasmuch as it has been mistakenly construed as providing some solace to the Arab boycott imposed on persons trading with Israel, the Navy will discontinue its use.[7]

Senator Clifford P. Case, Republican of New Jersey, greeted the Navy statement by saying:

As one who protested against the Navy Department's discriminatory policy in its oil shipping contracts, I warmly applaud the Navy's decision . . . to discontinue the use of its cancellation clause in future contracts. I hope the public protests which greeted revelation of this now discontinued practice will serve as notice to other Government agencies. The American public does not

[6] *New York Times*, January 20, 1960, p. 2.
[7] *Ibid.*, February 18, 1960.

believe a United States Government agency should knuckle under to any form of international blackmail.[8]

No doubt the American public does not like to see its government knuckling under to blackmail. In this case, however, the Navy would seem faced with the choice of losing large amounts of money if it happens to hire a tanker blacklisted by the Arabs, or of stopping its purchases of oil from an American company in Saudi Arabia. In practice the Navy probably will continue to ascertain that the ships it charters have had no previous dealings with Israel.

Also charged with discrimination in this respect are the Department of Agriculture and Commodity Credit Corporation. On February 4, 1960, the New York *Times* quoted shipping industry spokesmen in New York as saying that the two agencies explicitly forbid the shipment of U.S. government commodities to the United Arab Republic in vessels which have traded with Israel. Goods primarily involved were said to be cargoes of surplus farm products sold under the Public Law 480 program.

In a resolution February 28, 1960, the American Jewish Congress called on Congress to investigate these alleged discriminatory practices on the part of United States government agencies. The resolution also charged the State Department with having entered into "a gentleman's agreement" with Pakistan not to assign Americans of Jewish faith to diplomatic or other posts in that country. This was in addition, the resolution said, to the Defense Department's "admitted" accession to Saudi Arabian requests that no Jewish personnel be assigned to the United States air base at Dhahran.

[8] *Ibid.*, Feb. 18, 1960.

The allegation concerning Pakistan was denied flatly by State Department spokesman Lincoln White. With respect to Saudi Arabia, Mr. White pointed out that the Dhahran airfield belonged to Saudi Arabia, and that the air base facilities granted to the U.S. were of "considerable importance to our national security." Mr. White went on to say that the agreement covering the base stipulated that all personnel assigned there must be in possession of Saudi Arabian visas. He stated:

The Saudi Arabian Government in exercise of its sovereign right to legislate and control internal matters has normally refused to issue entry visas to persons of Jewish faith irrespective of nationality.

In doing so it states that this is a security precaution flowing directly from the continuing Arab-Israeli conflict.

The United States does not condone discriminatory action by foreign governments against its citizens on grounds of race or creed and it makes every continuing effort to eliminate through friendly means all such practices.[9]

Now it was Israel, or more specifically Zionist agencies in the United States, which were charging the U.S. government with conscious or unconscious favoritism toward the Arabs. In earlier years it had been all the other way around; the Arabs had accused the United States of favoritism toward Israel. By the spring of 1960 most Arab leaders appeared willing to go along with America's present degree of association with Israel, though the Arabic press continued to take swipes at this relationship.

Two further incidents underlined America's extreme difficulty in trying to maintain friendship with both Arabs and Israelis. Before approving the administration's foreign

[9] As quoted by Reuters in Washington, February 29, 1960.

aid bill for 1960-61, both Houses of Congress wrote in an amendment giving the President discretionary authority to withhold aid from the United Arab Republic until Cairo opened the Suez Canal to Israeli shipping. Though the protagonists were not mentioned by name, the amendment ,permitted the President to withhold foreign aid from any country engaged in economic warfare against any other nation receiving United States aid. Senate sponsors of the amendment, principally Kenneth B. Keating, New York Republican, and Paul H. Douglas, Democrat of Illinois, said this was the least Congress should do to protest the U.A.R.'s restrictions on ships serving Israel.

Opposing the Senate amendment, Senator J. William Fulbright, Arkansas Democrat and chairman of the Senate Foreign Relations Committee, told his colleagues that the amendment amounted to "political coercion by the United States on behalf of one side to the long-smouldering Arab-Israeli dispute. It contemplates that the President is to use the Mutual Security Act as a club to force the United Arab Republic to open the Suez Canal to Israeli shipping."[10]

Senator Fulbright was strongly backed up by the State Department. Mr. Fulbright read to the Senate a letter he had received from Douglas Dillon, Under Secretary of State, in which Mr. Dillon said the amendment would be widely interpreted as "favoritism for Israel" and a threat to use foreign aid as an instrument of political coercion. Mr. Dillon went on to say the amendment not only would incur the deep resentment of the Arab nations but also of their friends, the African and Asian states.

Despite these protests, the restrictive amendment was written into the foreign aid bill which received President

[10] As reported by Reuters in Washington, May 7, 1960.

Eisenhower's signature on May 16, 1960. Signing the bill, the President said he regretted the inclusion of the amendment aimed at the U.A.R. Since the amendment is discretionary only, the President very likely will ignore it and the United Arab Republic will continue to receive American aid. But the amendment remains on paper as the sense of the Congress that the United States should use its aid as a weapon in the Arab-Israeli dispute.

More immediate in its results was a second anti-Arab incident which began in New York on April 13, 1960. On that day a picket line was thrown around the U.A.R. ship "Cleopatra" in New York harbor by the Seafarers International Union. This picket line was respected by the International Longshoremen's Association, which refused to unload the Egyptian ship. Paul Hall, head of the S.I.U., termed the picketing a retaliation for the loss of U.S. seamen's jobs as a result of the Arab boycott of Israel. Rather than have their ships blacklisted by the Arabs, Mr. Hall asserted, some ship owners refused to trade with Israel, while others, whose vessels were already blacklisted, refused to transit the Suez Canal. The union leader also claimed American seamen had been harassed in Arab ports.

Senator Fulbright again took the lead in deploring what he termed the intrusion of private groups into the foreign policy function of the United States government. In a speech before the Senate April 25, Senator Fulbright declared:

The ostensible reason for this activity (picketing of the Cleopatra) was that the unions by this demonstration protest the action of the United Arab Republic in boycotting ships that have traded with Israel or called at Israeli ports.

I hold no brief for U.A.R. interference with international traffic passing through the Suez Canal. The point is, however, that the

U.S. Government is proceeding through diplomatic channels to promote free passage through the canal. The Israeli Government, which complains that the U.A.R. stops its ships, has available to it the procedures of the United Nations as well as other diplomatic devices for urging its views on the government of the U.A.R. Yet, despite the official actions of the United States, we find private groups proceeding by coercive devices of their own to interfere with the official activities of our government in the field of foreign policy.[11]

On April 29 Senator Fulbright, again speaking to the Senate, coupled the Keating-Douglas amendment with the "Cleopatra" picketing as "part of a pattern which I find disastrous to the functioning of our constitutional system . . . In what is probably the most delicate international situation which exists in the world today, 180,000,000 Americans find their foreign policy being whipsawed by an irresponsible maritime union and by a minority pressure group."[12]

While owners of the "Cleopatra"—the Khedivial Mail Line of Alexandria—unsuccessfully sought to end the picketing through the United States courts, Arab trade unions took matters into their own hands. Meeting in Cairo, the International Federation of Arab Trade Unions decreed a boycott of American flag ships in all Arab ports, from the Atlantic to the Persian Gulf, effective from April 29 until the "Cleopatra" picketing ended.

The boycott was completely enforced. Privately the U.A.R. and Lebanese governments urged the United States to divert American ships from their ports in order to prevent incidents. The two Arab governments indicated their willingness to bear the costs involved in switching

---

[11] Quoted by the United States Information Service Wireless Bulletin of April 26, 1960.
[12] New York Times, April 29, 1960.

cargoes from American to non-American ships in non-Arab Mediterranean ports.

As anti-American feeling rose in the Arab world, the White House appealed to American labor leaders to work out a formula to end the picketing. The great concern was that the old image of "American-Zionist conspiracy," which the Eisenhower administration had worked so hard to dispel, once again would become fixed in Arab thought. Already Arab newspapers and leaders, including President Nasser, were branding the "Cleopatra" picketing a "Zionist-imperialist" plot against the Arabs.

The White House appeal achieved no immediate results. George Meany, America's top labor leader, said after conferring with U.S. Secretary of Labor James Mitchell that the picketing of the "Cleopatra" was a protest against indignities suffered by American seamen in Arab ports. Earlier Mr. Hall, of the Seafarers International Union, had denied that any outside influence was present in the picketing. Mr. Meany, president of the American Federation of Labor-Congress of Industrial Organizations, said he disagreed with Senator Fulbright that the picketing was a political act.

Meanwhile, everyone was losing and no one was gaining from the storm aroused. Hungry Syrians, enduring their third straight year of drought, had been promised 5,000 tons of emergency wheat shipments by the Syrian branch of the U.A.R. government. At the same time American vessels bringing Public Law 480 wheat to Syria were being diverted from the Syrian port of Latakia because Syrian dockers refused to unload them. American tourists, some of whom may have saved for a lifetime for a Mediterranean cruise, were unable to land at Lebanese and U.A.R. ports.

American maritime unions, protesting the loss of U.S. seafaring jobs because of the anti-Israel boycott, were threatened with far greater job loss from the Arab boycott of American flag ships. In India, the Bombay Port Trust General Workers Union pledged to close Bombay to American shipping unless the "Cleopatra" picketing was stopped. Nor could the American unions by their picketing hope to achieve their avowed goal of ending Arab restrictions against ships dealing with Israel. Instead, Arab unions were carrying out their promise to return two blows for every one dealt to an Arab ship by American workers.

Israel, too, was concerned, lest the American public connect the Zionists with the "Cleopatra" affair and turn its resentment against the Jewish state. American Zionists disclaimed any link with the picketing. Nonetheless, some Israeli officials privately expressed their fear that this disclaimer might be overridden in the American people's thought by the obviously anti-Arab character of the picketing.

These factors, plus the urgent desire of the United States government to end the new boycott before Arab-American cooperation was destroyed, broke the stalemate. On May 6 the Seafarers International Union ended its picketing in return for a State Department promise to take new steps to halt the blacklisting of American ships by Arab governments. The formula was drawn up only after involved negotiation among Douglas Dillon, as Acting Secretary of State, Labor Secretary James Mitchell, Mr. Meany, and Arthur J. Goldberg, A.F.L.-C.I.O. special counsel.

Specifically, the State Department committed itself to consult with the A.F.L.-C.I.O. and its maritime unions on "future developments affecting American vessels and seamen" in the Middle East. Mr. Dillon also assured the unions that the State Department would "undertake to investigate fully the grievances of the Seafarers International Union and, through appropriate diplomatic action with the foreign countries involved, to renew its efforts to assure freedom of the seas and to protect the interests of our shipping and seamen now being discriminated against by the Arab boycott and blacklisting policy."[13]

What the State Department could do that would prove effective was not clear. In an earlier press conference President Eisenhower had said he saw no way but the use of force to open the Suez Canal to Israeli shipping, and the United States certainly was not going to try that. Yet Paul Hall, president of the S.I.U., warned that picketing of Arab ships would be resumed unless the State Department gave "practical implementation" to its pledge to investigate the union's complaints. The U.S. government had been given the prickly task of trying to preserve Arab-American friendship while putting enough pressure on the Arabs to prevent American maritime unions from putting up their picket lines again.

In the Middle East, Arab stevedores promptly began working American ships, amid general rejoicing that Arab "unity and solidarity" had foiled a new "Zionist plot" against the Arabs. In a speech in New York on May 8 Hafik Asha, U.A.R. representative in the United Nations, summed up the Arab viewpoint by terming the "Cleopatra" picketing "a provocative, malicious, and sinister act" by Israel and Zionism. It was, Mr. Asha said, "another attempt by Israel and Zionism to undermine the improved

13 *New York Times*, May 8, 1960.

relations between the United States and the United Arab Republic."[14]

If nothing else, the whole affair proved that the United States could cultivate friendship and cooperation with both Arabs and Israelis only through the utmost skill and flexibility.

All this brought Israel no nearer her own goal of free passage through the Suez Canal, nor did it diminish Israel's sense that her Arab neighbors were growing more implacable toward her. Vis-à-vis the Arabs, Israel had chalked up only one major gain since the Suez campaign of 1956. That was unrestricted use of the Gulf of Aqaba for Israeli shipping, guaranteed by the presence of the United Nations Emergency Force at the southern tip of the Sinai Peninsula. As a result, Israel's southern port of Elath was booming as the country's new trade outlet to east Africa and the Far East. Apart from this, Israel felt herself surrounded by enemies who were steadily growing stronger economically and militarily.

There was independent evidence to support Israel's contention that the Arabs were in no mood to compromise with the Jewish state. Part of this evidence centered on the attitude of the one million Palestine Arab refugees, who now have been separated from their homeland for twelve years.

The younger generation of refugees, increasingly taking over leadership of the refugee groups, is beginning to demand a harder policy toward Israel than the Arab governments have been employing. One Palestinian refugee leader—who has spent years in the United States as an Arab spokesman—said privately he now thinks he was naive

[14] *Ibid.*, May 8, 1960.

to believe in the possibility of a peaceful settlement of the Palestine dispute.

Talks with young refugees and visits to refugee camps since he returned to the Middle East have convinced him that this possibility may have disappeared. Involved in this judgment is not only the activist attitude of younger refugees but also general Arab confidence that time is working on the Arab side; that Arab capabilities are growing; that the Arab side of the case is better understood in the West than it was in the past; and that Jews in the United States are bound to grow weary of the exhausting financial effort to keep Israel afloat.

The newest element in this picture is the growing political activity of the refugees themselves. Various refugee groups have pooled their activities in a new organization called the Palestine Arab Congress under the chairmanship of Dr. Fayez Sayegh, a Palestinian well-known in the United States as an Arab League information official.

In assessing the degree of influence the refugees can exercise on Arab policy, one should recall that refugees registered with the United Nations Relief and Works Agency (UNRWA) form more than two-thirds of the total population of the Gaza Strip; 56 per cent of Jordan's population; and nearly 10 per cent of Lebanon's population.[15] With the refugee attitude continuing to harden, it does not seem that as a generation which knew the old days in Palestine disappears, the problem will tend to be solved.

An estimated 20 per cent of the refugees who actually lived in Palestine have already died. Yet bitterness still

[15] On January 1, 1960, the total of refugees registered with and assisted by the United Nations Relief and Works Agency for Palestine Refugees (UNRWA) was as follows: 251,976 in the Gaza Strip; 604,236 in Jordan; 134,569 in Lebanon; and 112,949 in Syria, for a grand total of 1,103,730.

rides the others when they think of their homeland. As part
of their drawing lessons refugee children are given maps
of Palestine to color—Palestine as it was when it belonged
to the Arabs, not as it is today. A curious byproduct of
this refugee fixation is the fact that a refugee child born
in Syria, for example, will say: "I am from such and such
a town in Palestine," though he speaks with a Syrian dia-
lect and never has seen the town he calls home.

A striking example of the attitude of refugee children
was provided a recent visitor to a United Nations Relief
and Works Agency school in Syria, where he was given
an impromptu show by seven refugee girls. Three of the
girls, each wearing a crown on her head, stood on one side
and named themselves "Haifa," "Jaffa," and "Acre," three
Israeli-occupied towns. Three others stood opposite and
named themselves "Hebron," "Jericho," and "Nablus,"
three Palestinian towns now in the Hashemite kingdom of
Jordan. The oldest girl stood in the center and called herself "Damascus."

"Haifa" began dancing and reciting that her beautiful
blue Mediterranean Sea awaited liberation. "Hebron" responded in poetry that she was waiting to help "Haifa"
gain her freedom. "Jaffa" spoke of her orange groves, and
"Jericho" replied. "Acre" lamented that once she had been
a mighty fortress which had stopped Napoleon, but now
was occupied by the enemy. "Nablus" responded as the
protector, awaiting the chance to help. Then "Damascus"
chimed in that her army, her men, were at the service of
the conquered towns, to help them regain their liberty.

The fact that most Arabs are united in opposition to
Israel does not mean there is no friction between Palestine
Arabs and their hosts of the past twelve years. Despite pub-
lic protestations to the contrary, there tends to be rivalry

between the refugees and the other Arabs among whom they live.

Lebanese merchants in Beirut deplore the fact that Hamra Street, shopping center of suburban Beirut, is lined with the shops of Palestinians, drawing business away from the older stores downtown. This is part of the general Arab complaint that those Palestinians who managed to take some money with them when they fled, or who had bank accounts outside Palestine, tend, because of their superior education and business experience under the British mandate, to outdo other Arabs competitively. Lebanese and Syrian laborers, "pick and shovel" workers, resent the fact that refugees from the camps can offer their labor more cheaply, because they receive a monthly food ration from UNRWA.

The refugees themselves complain of discrimination against them, even in a country such as Syria where officially there is equality of work opportunity between refugees and Syrians. Some time ago, for example, Communist bloc countries offered a number of technical scholarships to Syrian youth. Palestinians were allowed to compete and a number of them won. Their names were published, but then they were told: "You are granted equality of job opportunity under our Syrian law, but not equality of scholarship opportunity." So they were denied the scholarships, though the later hue and cry eventually caused Syrian officials to reverse their stand.

Conversely, refugee children in Syria are guaranteed at least a primary education in UNRWA schools. An equivalent opportunity does not exist for all Syrian children, particularly those who live in remote villages or in desert tents.

On another occasion a number of Palestinian secondary school graduates in Gaza applied for permission to enter the Syrian University in Damascus. Egyptian universities were already full. When the boys arrived in Damascus, they thronged UNRWA offices, saying that what they really wanted was work, which they could not obtain in overcrowded Gaza. When Syrian officials learned this, the boys were sent back to Gaza, on the grounds they were foreigners. Gaza, it was claimed, was not a part of the United Arab Republic, though under the control and protection of Egypt.

These are examples of the sense of separation which many Palestinians feel. Living apart as they do, in a kind of ghetto existence, it is hard for them to make friends and normal contacts among other Arabs. In whichever country they live, they feel something is lacking. In Lebanon, where unemployment is a problem, sharp restrictions are put upon their permission to work. In Syria they have job opportunity, but no citizenship. In Jordan they are citizens, but have little opportunity to work.

These internal differences among the Arabs are of scant benefit to Israel, since they do not break through the monolithic front of hostility which the Arabs present to the Jewish state. To many Israelis it seems utterly unrealistic of the Arabs not to accept Israeli technical help in improving Arab agriculture and industry. Israel has "Point Four" missions of her own operating in a number of African and Asian countries, including Ghana, Burma, and Iran. Why not among the Arabs, the Israelis ask, even as they realize that the last thing a proud and sensitive Arab wants is to be helped by the man he has been taught to call an enemy.

The fact is that Arab economies, boosted in part by the technical and economic help of the United States, are slowly improving on their own. So is the ability of the

Arabs to use the modern arms they have obtained from the Russians. Unfortunately, this burgeoning self-confidence is accompanied by zeal among many Arabs to "get back" at Israel as soon as the Arabs are strong enough. This attitude causes many Israelis to be bitterly resentful of conscious American attempts to improve United States relations with President Nasser's U.A.R., most powerful of the Arab states.

I have visited Israeli kibbutzim, or communal villages, near Arab frontiers, where the best-built edifice in the kibbutz was the concrete air raid shelter to which children could be rushed should Arab gunfire come down from the hills. I have been told of the nightly anguish of Jewish mothers during the years when Arab commandos crept through the armistice lines in Sinai to raid Israeli settlements. Though it is a fact unrelated to the Arab-Israeli dispute, some of these mothers carried blue tattoo marks pricked into their skins in Nazi concentration camps.

I recall the former American girl I met in a kibbutz near the Gaza Strip. In response to my astonished, perhaps naive, question as to why she had changed her citizenship, she looked at me flatly. "I wouldn't say I felt out of place in the United States," she said, "but I never felt wholly at home." She had been born and brought up in a tough section of New York City, she went on, a district inhabited largely by Italians, Irish, and Jews. Whenever an argument arose between her and children of other racial backgrounds, she was called a "dirty Yid." In Israel she was among her own kind; she felt at peace and at home, despite the dangers to which her new homeland was exposed. She was a girl who had been to Zionist camps in the United States, and who had experienced Zionist indoctrination for as long as she could remember.

There are others like her in Israel, and others, perhaps many others, still in the United States. To Jews such as these, both in Israel and America, it is just as painful to watch the United States strengthening Arab leaders and lands, as it is for the Arabs to know that American aid flows to the Jewish state.

# CHAPTER 6

# American Interests in the Middle East

What are American interests in the Middle East? There is no dearth of official definition, for in 1959 President Eisenhower, William M. Rountree, then Assistant Secretary of State for Near Eastern and South Asian Affairs, and Parker K. Hart, deputy to Mr. Rountree, all expressed themselves on the subject. In a press conference in Washington May 4, 1959, Mr. Eisenhower declared the United States was trying to show Middle Eastern countries they had a better chance of achieving their aspirations in freedom than through association with the Soviets.[1] The President further said the United States intended to be fair to all nations in the area, sought not to promote quarrels, nor to boost the prestige of anyone.

In testimony before the Senate Foreign Relations Committee May 14, 1959, Assistant Secretary of State Rountree

[1] As reported by the Associated Press, May 5, 1959.

said that United States aid programs in the Middle East were designed "to support the development of strong and independent nations able and willing to resist the subversive efforts of international communism."[2] Mr. Rountree went on to list other aims of U.S. policy in the area as follows:

Second, to contribute, if requested by the nations of the area, to their security, recognizing that in a broad sense their security is our security;

Third, to assist and encourage the countries of the area to resolve their disputes in accordance with the principles of the Charter of the United Nations;

Fourth, to contribute to the economic progress and development of the nations of the Near East and South Asia.[3]

In testimony given on August 13, 1959, before the Senate Appropriations Committee in Washington, Parker K. Hart repeated almost verbatim the same policy goals outlined earlier by his chief, Mr. Rountree.

From this it will be seen that top officials of the United States government regard the containment of communism as America's paramount goal in the Middle East. The Middle East itself is deeply important, because of its primacy as a source of oil and because it contains almost indispensable sea, air, and land routes for Western trade with the world east of Suez. Communist control of the Arab Middle East would place in constant jeopardy the West's supply of Middle Eastern oil, important to the United States and vital to Britain and Western Europe. Likewise, Communist control of the area would threaten with political interruptions the trans-Suez trade which is vital to America's Western allies, though less so to the

[2] As reported by the United States Information Service Wireless Bulletin of May 15, 1959.
[3] *Ibid.*, August 13, 1959.

United States itself since much of America's trade with Asia is carried on from the United States' west coast or through the Panama Canal.

Finally, Communist domination of the Middle East would cut America's defense links running from the North Atlantic Treaty Organization in Europe, through the Central Treaty Organization (Turkey, Iran, and Pakistan among Asian states), to the Southeast Asia Treaty Organization.

These are reasons why it is considered vital to preserve the Middle East as a non-Communist part of the world. But quite apart from its own intrinsic importance, the Middle East is a land bridge connecting Europe with Asia and Africa. Soviet conquest of Iran or Iraq, for example, whether directly or through subversion by local Communists, would afford the U.S.S.R. access to the Persian Gulf and Indian Ocean, thus turning the flank of Pakistan and India.

The great continent of Africa is a cockpit of emergent nationalism in which anti-colonialism—which is to say, anti-Westernism—threatens to run rampant as one colony after another either struggles toward or achieves independence. Particularly damaging to the white West is the bitter struggle between Frenchman and Arab in Algeria, and the equally intense rivalry between Negro and white in the Union of South Africa. Between these extremes runs a gamut of African colonial problems involving Britain, France, and other European powers.

To countless Africans the West symbolizes the hated foreign presence, while the Soviet Union remains an unknown quantity verbally championing the very goals for which Africans are striving. In the struggle to keep new African nations non-Communist—anti-Communist is perhaps more than can be hoped for—the West urgently needs the insulation of at least a "neutral" Middle East. A pro-Communist Arab world, or even a pro-Communist Egypt, would greatly simplify the Soviets' task of seeking to indoctrinate Africans. The converse also is true, and the example of President Nasser's war of attrition against Arab communism presumably is not lost on many African leaders.

All these are key reasons why the United States regards the preservation of a non-Communist Middle East, with the encouragement of anti-Communist pockets wherever possible, as its paramount goal in the area. It seems accurate to say the United States would fight rather than lose the Middle East to the Communists, unless the process of loss involved a subversion so gradual and apparently legal that no handle was provided which the United States could grasp and declare "thus far and no farther."

Middle Eastern oil might seem of only indirect concern to the United States, since only about four per cent of America's total petroleum consumption is imported from the Middle East. But this figure does not reflect actual American demand for Arab oil. Rather it has been imposed by the United States government at the urging of independent oil producers in the United States, grouped in the Independent Producers Association of America.

This organization argues that every barrel of foreign oil imported cuts a barrel from domestic production under the network of production controls erected by federal and state regulatory agencies. In effect these agencies determine monthly the rate of petroleum demand throughout the United States and then share out among domestic companies the production necessary to meet this demand. To prevent cheaper foreign oil—cheaper because of lower production costs—from cutting too deeply into these monthly quotas, the United States government at first urged voluntary import restrictions on the industry. However, on March 12, 1959, mandatory import controls were substituted by the government under the "peril point" clause of the Reciprocal Trade Agreement. Under these controls the importation of Arab oil into the United States is strictly limited.

All this is somewhat beside the point in measuring the importance of Middle Eastern oil to the United States. There is first the enormous investment of American companies in the area, amounting to billions of dollars. American interests own 100 per cent of the producing company in Saudi Arabia; 50 per cent of the Kuwait Oil Company; 23.75 per cent of production in Iraq; 100 per cent of the Bahrein Petroleum Company; 23.75 per cent of production in Qatar; and 40 per cent of the international Consortium in Iran, plus interests in smaller operations elsewhere in the Middle East.

Overriding even this in importance is the fact that the main burden of supplying Europe's essential oil needs would fall on the United States if Middle Eastern supplies were cut off. This was the case during the Suez crisis of 1956, when blockade of the Suez Canal by Egypt and sabotage of the Iraq Petroleum Company's pipeline in Syria cost Western Europe about 70 per cent of its normal supplies. Even by pressing all available tankers into service on the long haul around the tip of Africa, Europe still would have been at least 45 per cent short of its usual supplies.[4]

[4] For a more complete discussion of this question see George Lenczowski, *Oil and State in the Middle East* (Ithaca: Cornell University Press, 1960), Part Five.

Into this breach stepped the United States through the agency of the Middle East Emergency Committee, a coalition of 15 American oil companies specifically exempted by the United States government from antitrust legislation. By increasing daily western hemisphere production at the rate of 725,000 barrels in the United States, 50,000 barrels in Venezuela, and 25,000 barrels in Canada, the Emergency Committee made up most, though not all, of Europe's deficit. For the rest Europe was forced to rely on rationing and allocation of oil to essential uses. Though this imposed no real strain on western hemisphere productive capacity, already far in excess of normal daily output, its real cost lay in the outflow of hard currency with which Europe had to pay for this oil.

A prolonged deprivation of Middle Eastern oil would impose such a drain on European treasuries that in the long run the deficit almost certainly would be transferred to the United States Treasury, which in some form would have to advance loans to Europe to pay for western hemisphere oil. There is also the point that western hemisphere reserves would be sucked away to a degree considered unsafe by American defense planners.

For all these reasons the importance attached by the United States to the continued flow of Arab oil can hardly be overestimated. The question then arises: how long into the future is Europe's demand for Middle Eastern oil likely to continue?

At this writing the world is experiencing a glut of crude oil production, causing the lay up of hundreds of tankers and the depression of oil prices generally. Also, Saharan and Libyan oil, which to some extent will compete with Middle Eastern oil, as yet have not made their full entry into the world market. Judgments vary as to the effect

North African oil will have on Middle East production. The Arab producing countries tend to minimize the possible effects, while some Western sources hint at replacement of Middle Eastern oil with output from North Africa, partly, perhaps, to warn Arab governments against seeking contract improvements. France in particular appears determined to force refineries operating in France to buy Saharan crude, either to refine themselves or to ship to affiliates elsewhere. Since 90 per cent of France's current crude requirements come from the Middle East, the substitution of Saharan oil for French internal consumption certainly will have an adverse effect on the Middle East.

Light Saharan oil is unsuited to the French market's demand for heavy products. Thus international refining companies operating in France may be forced to send their allotment of Saharan crude to their refineries in the western hemisphere, in place of the Middle Eastern oil they now send. They then would continue to use heavier Middle Eastern crude in their French refineries. But the net effect would be a drop in the use of Middle Eastern oil corresponding exactly to the amount of Saharan oil produced, whether refined in France or elsewhere.

Libya's contribution to the total picture is even more uncertain, since Libyan reserves of heavy crude—exempt from the perils of Suez Canal passage—may prove to rival those of Kuwait, estimated at 60,000,000,000 barrels. Another unsettling factor is the fact that the Soviet Union, which already daily sells 300,000 barrels of its own oil in western Europe, is striving to enlarge its share of this market.

In other words, petroleum experts themselves have formed no unanimous opinion as to the effect on Middle Eastern production of the new North African finds. Leaving aside the extremes of opinion, the indication is that North African oil may possibly supply the world's annual increase in demand, now running in the range of 7 per cent, leaving Middle Eastern production totals roughly at their current levels.

On one thing the experts seem clear. As far into the future as one can project, Middle Eastern oil will be a necessity to the free world. As one American oil executive put it: "We could get along without any one producing country, but not without the Middle East as a whole. Much of the equipment needed for extracting oil shales and tar sands, on which we would have to fall back if we lost the Middle East, has yet to be designed."

A recent authoritative estimate places total free world demand for oil in 1975 at 40,000,000 barrels a day, compared with today's free world consumption of about 17,000,000 barrels daily. Another equally authoritative estimate says that if by the year 2000 one third of the world's total energy requirements is met by atomic energy, world demand for oil still will be four times as great as it is today.

When it is realized that of the world's total proven reserves of 37,000,000,000 metric tons, the Middle East has 23,900,000,000 tons, it will be seen that this area will remain very important for many years to come. Even this is not the whole story, oil experts point out, since probable reserves are at least triple the total of proven reserves, and the Middle East may possess as much as 90 per cent of the world's probable reserves.

Another legitimate American interest in the Middle East is to help build up Arab and other local economies through technical and economic aid wherever such help may be sought. Though the betterment of living conditions for indigent peoples is worthy in itself, the benefits of such a program go beyond altruism. The Arab Middle East is groping through a protracted period of social ferment, brought on largely by the impact of Western education and technology on younger elements of Arab society. This jarring impact has served to turn these elements—army officers, doctors, lawyers, teachers, and others—against the age-old *status quo* in the Arab world, under which a tight oligarchy of wealthy land-owning families almost literally enslaved the great mass of Arab peasantry.

A feature of this mental ferment is anti-Westernism, fostered partly because the Arabs were denied independence by the French and British mandates between the two world wars, and partly because the Western powers often have appeared to support the *status quo*. This anti-Westernism was not lessened by the fact that the new Arab devotion to republicanism and social reform sprang frequently from seeds planted by British and American educators throughout the Middle East.

Within this over-all process of ferment, Egypt and Syria already have experienced their revolts against the past, while Iraq is undergoing at least one phase of hers. The weight of logic indicates that similar revolutions must be expected at some time in Jordan and Saudi Arabia, not to mention the more primitive sheikdoms along the Persian Gulf.

Here the United States must proceed with the utmost care, since clearly America is a major factor of support behind the existing regimes both in Saudi Arabia and Jordan. American aid to Jordan is designed largely to prevent the collapse of King Hussein's government and the advent of chaos; in Saudi Arabia the American purpose is to forge a cooperative link between the Saudi Arab government and the Arabian American Oil Company, and to preserve United States Air Force base rights at Dhahran.

Arab nationalists, or at least the more mature of them, understand and to some extent accept American aid to the Arab kings. They might not so accept it, however, if the United States were not also manifestly ready to help the new military regimes with their development programs. This is one reason for the importance of Point Four aid and economic subsidies to the United Arab Republic, the Sudan, and eventually to Iraq, if and when that nation settles down at least to a neutralism receptive of American help.

President Nasser is the leading example of an Arab revolutionary who, once in power, faced staggering problems that had to be solved before he could implement the promises he had made to his people. Failure to solve his economic and social problems, or at least to keep pace with their growth, would mean either the foundering of Mr. Nasser's government or his reversion to outside adventures to mask his frustrations at home. It is hard to see how anyone but the Communists, and possibly Israel, could gain from either eventuality.

Here it is that American technical and economic help, designed to ease Cairo and Damascus over crisis points in their development, can play an important role in maintaining stability within the U.A.R. To an extent the same is true of American aid in every other country of the Middle East where United States help is welcomed. American support programs form essential steps toward the long-range goal of Arab national self-confidence based on economic and social security at home, and without which there can be no true stability in the Middle East.

Almost certainly Arab leaders could not rejuvenate their

societies without help from the major industrialized powers. Failure of the United States to give aid would mean America's abdication of a legitimate self-interest in the Middle East, and the advancement of Soviet interests in the area.

To promote its manifold concerns in the Middle East, the United States has no formal treaty alliances either with Israel or with any Arab power, except for specific agreements allowing American forces to use airfields in Saudi Arabia and Libya. This lack of treaties is by design, since events have made it painfully clear to American leaders that the Arabs emphatically reject the concept of pacts and that a bilateral association between Israel and the United States would wreck Arab-American cooperation.

This knowledge came only after Secretary of State Dulles sought twice to enlist Arab support for Western alliances directed against the Soviet Union. The first attempt was through the Baghdad Pact, sponsored by Britain and the United States early in 1955 and designed to erect a screen along the Soviet Union's southern border to prevent the latter's expansion southward. Insofar as the Arabs and United States were concerned, the Baghdad Pact boomeranged badly.

Only Iraq among Arab states joined, while Egypt led most of the rest of the Arab world in condemning this Western-sponsored alliance. To be sure, narrow Egyptian interests formed part of this opposition, since Cairo preferred an Arab defensive alliance within the Arab League, which Egypt could dominate. Beyond this, however, a majority of Arab leaders interpreted the Baghdad Pact as a Western device to perpetuate British and American control of the Arab world and to distract the Arabs from the Palestine problem by conjuring up the threat of Communist imperialism from the north.

This situation worsened in December, 1955, when Britain tried to persuade Jordan to join the Baghdad Pact in return for the promise of jet planes and heavy armor for Jordan's Arab Legion. Angry demonstrations throughout Jordan forced King Hussein to repudiate any desire to join the Baghdad Pact. Also set in motion was a train of events leading to the expulsion of Glubb Pasha as commander of the Arab Legion and the abrogation in 1957 of the Anglo-Jordanian treaty of 1948, under which Britain had subsidized the economic stability of Jordan. It was Jordan's breaking of this treaty which led to the substitution of American for British subsidy in Jordan.

Even Iraq was held within the Baghdad Pact only by the strong hand of Premier Nuri es-Said. On March 24, 1959—seven months after he swept Nuri into oblivion—Iraqi Premier Abdel Karim Kassem withdrew his country from the Baghdad Pact. The organization then renamed itself the Central Treaty Organization, embracing Britain, Turkey, Iran, and Pakistan. The United States, though a sponsor of the alliance, never had joined the Baghdad Pact beyond membership in certain of its key committees.

Though still declining to become a full member of the Central Treaty Organization, the United States soothed the alliance's uneasy Asian members by signing bilateral treaties with Turkey, Iran, and Pakistan, guaranteeing American help in the event any one of these nations was attacked. Though the wording was left vague, presumably this meant aggression by a Communist power, since the treaties stipulated American help would come under the umbrella of the Eisenhower Doctrine.

Clearly the Baghdad Pact had been a failure for American policy in the Arab world. Not only had the alliance aroused intense opposition among most Arabs, but the

Soviet Union had leapfrogged over the Baghdad Pact through its arms deals with Egypt and Syria. Very likely, through those original deals and its subsequent economic agreements with the U.A.R., the Soviets are every inch as far into the Middle East as though the Baghdad Pact never had existed.

Some good is being done by improving the communications and transportation network among Turkey, Iran, and Pakistan, and an alliance of these states with the United States and Britain against the Soviet Union is a positive step. But all this could have been achieved without seeking to include any Arab country in the Baghdad Pact.

In fairness to Mr. Dulles it should be pointed out that his original concept appeared to be an alliance of those Middle Eastern states bordering the Soviet Union, plus Iraq, whose northern oil fields lie close to Soviet territory. It was the British who sought to "thicken" the pact by including other Arab states.

The United States' second attempt to elicit a formal anti-Communist expression from the Arabs was the so-called Eisenhower Doctrine, approved by Congress in March, 1957. This doctrine was an attempt to establish an acceptable basis for American intervention to halt Communist penetration of the Middle East. Thus the President received authorization from Congress to send United States forces to the help of any Mideastern nation attacked by a power under the control of international communism—if the victim requested American help. A second arm of the Eisenhower Doctrine offered economic aid to any Middle Eastern country willing to cooperate in the fight against communism.

While this may sound innocuous, even magnanimous, to American ears, it was not so interpreted by Arab leaders pledged to a neutralist philosophy. To such leaders, notably in Egypt, Syria, today's Iraq, and to some extent in Saudi Arabia, the doctrine smacked of dependence on the United States and the gradual submersion of Arab sovereignty beneath a new type of Western control. Thus the Eisenhower Doctrine was formally endorsed only by the Lebanese government of President Camille Chamoun. The government which replaced Mr. Chamoun after the Lebanese rebellion of 1958 has sought to give the impression that the Eisenhower Doctrine no longer exists as an issue requiring either approval or repudiation. Iraq, still under Nuri es-Said at the time, joined with the other Baghdad Pact powers in approving the Eisenhower Doctrine, but this approval vanished along with Nuri's government itself.

The Eisenhower Doctrine remains on the books as an approved piece of legislation at the President's service. But talk of the doctrine has been notably muted since the passing of Mr. Dulles and his replacement by Secretary of State Christian A. Herter. It now is thought in Washington that more in the way of Arab-American cooperation can be achieved without requiring formal anti-Communist and pro-American commitments on the part of Arab leaders.

Indeed it is difficult to imagine a single Arab chief of state in the Middle East who today would endorse the Eisenhower Doctrine, despite the fact some of these leaders undoubtedly would accept American help in the event of actual attack by a Communist power. As for economic aid, the United Arab Republic, Lebanon, and Jordan already are receiving as much United States help as they would derive from adherence to the Eisenhower Doctrine.

Thus America's formal treaties with Middle Eastern powers are confined to its bilateral treaties with Turkey, Iran, and Pakistan, plus the air base agreements with Saudi

Arabia and Libya. Not to be counted as treaties are Washington's periodic economic and technical aid agreements. Israel's evident desire for a bilateral defense treaty similar to that obtained by the CENTO powers has been frustrated by the Arab-Israeli dispute.

In every direction American policy toward the Middle East today tends to be more flexible and freer from arbitrary targets of achievement than at any time since the Palestine war of 1948. In this process of normalization the United States had a legacy of good will on which to draw among many Arabs, a legacy which has been largely obscured, though not wholly dissipated, by events since 1948.

Over a period of many years this good will was sown by American educators, usually in the service of various Protestant missions, who came to the Arab world beginning in the latter part of the nineteenth century and established schools in Lebanon, Syria, and Palestine. Though the most famous of these institutions is the American University of Beirut, there are literally dozens of other American-founded schools for Arab boys and girls, through which have been funneled thousands of Arabs who today lead their nations in government, business, and the professions.

In their American teachers at these schools Arab students met men and women who were principled, kindly, disinterested in politics, but passionately interested in the improvement of the individuals who came to them to learn. The impression made by these missionary educators was so pervasive and so uniformly favorable that after World War I the Arabs—who had known few other Americans at first hand—expressed their preference for an American mandate, if they had to have a Western mandate at all.

In general this pro-American sentiment among the Arabs prevailed up through the end of World War II and the emergence of the Arab-Jewish question. Had the United States shared the occupation of Arab lands with Britain and France between the two world wars, undoubtedly America would have become a target of anti-Western bitterness. But the United States was not so involved in the Middle East at that time; indeed, Washington's political and diplomatic role in the area became significant only when Britain and France, weakened by World War II, were forced to reduce their holdings in the Middle East. The resulting vacuum progressively was filled by the United States.

To translate American interests into specific cooperative arrangements with Middle Eastern countries inevitably involves the United States in a host of complex local problems. Can such and such a tract of Egyptian desert be irrigated to support fellahin from the Nile Valley? In view of the tariffs levied on Jordanian goods passing through Lebanon and Syria, should an all-weather road be built over the long desert route to Jordan's own port of Aqaba? How can Lebanese be taught to package their fruit so as to prevent spoilage and compete more favorably in foreign markets? How does one persuade sensitive Iranian officials that their army is receiving all the American equipment it can profitably absorb, when Turkish forces are getting more?

These are the kinds of problems on which Middle Easterners expect American advice and help. Technical advice and economic grants, offered tactfully and with an eye closed to a certain amount of wastage and even corruption, become the means of translating American interests into action in the Middle East.

Without participation in a nation's development United States interests could not be served. To make this participation seem nonintrusive, and yet yield lasting benefits to the nation concerned, requires technical and diplomatic skills of the highest order, since often age-old customs must be changed in the process. This being so, American technicians sometimes are forced to be content with a pitiful degree of progress compared with the amount of effort expended.

There is a great need for land reform, to choose one example, in most of the Middle East. Yet to distribute land to Arab or Iranian peasants runs squarely against a social pattern which was established before the United States was born. The recent history of Iranian land reform illustrates the stupendous task of lifting a nation by its bootstraps, and also throws light on the magnitude of local tangles in which American technicians become enmeshed when serving their government's interests overseas.

Recently Shah Reza Pahlevi visited a group of Iranian peasants who had been given public domain lands at Gonbad Kabous in Khorosan Province, near the Soviet frontier in northeastern Iran. These peasants had been sent to Germany for agricultural training and the monarch was anxious to see how they were progressing.

One farmer told the Shah all would be well if only he were given his legitimate share of irrigation water by his neighbor. The Shah asked who the neighbor was. The farmer knew him only by name. It turned out to be the Shah's personal adjutant. The adjutant lost his job and the peasant got his water.

The story describes both the Shah's determination to spread social reforms in his country and the resistance which the monarch meets from certain entrenched elements of Iranian society. It all adds up to an extremely complex affair and one difficult for many Westerners to comprehend, as they view the vast disparity between intention and practice in Iranian land reform.

On the surface land reform in Iran is simple to understand. It divides into three parts—the distribution of Crown lands (those belonging to the Shah), the distribution of public domain lands (those belonging to the government), and the cutting up of great private estates. The program involving Crown lands has progressed farthest; that involving public lands less far, while a law authorizing private land reform was passed by the Iranian Majlis (lower house of Parliament) only in March, 1960.

Here the simplicity ends and complexity begins. Iran has under cultivation about 6,000,000 hectares of land (one hectare equals 2.471 acres). There are at least 2,000,000 farm families in Iran. An equal distribution of cultivated land among these 2,000,000 families would give each one three hectares, not enough for subsistence when it is realized that at least two-thirds of Iran's farmland is dry-farmed. (Land that is dry-farmed depends on the vagaries of the rainfall. Wet farming makes use of irrigation.)

Adding to the scarcity of land and water is the fact that no clear body of land laws exists; ownership rights often are difficult to trace; and an enormous amount of survey and study work is needed merely to determine how to put each tract of land to most efficient use. A further need is to train up a body of "extension service" specialists able to operate peasants' cooperatives in the fields of crop care, credit establishment, and marketing.

These difficulties are faced in every phase of land reform —Crown, public domain, and private—in Iran.

Of the Crown's total holdings of cultivated land of about 500,000 hectares, supporting 50,000 families, approximately one half has been distributed to peasant families over the past three years. The enormous advantage here is that the Shah, as the owner, is urging on the distribution, in contrast to other owners who obstruct land reform where possible. Another great advantage is that the Shah plows back all revenues from land sales into the Omran (Development) Bank, an organization set up by the Shah to administer the distribution of his lands.

A peasant buys his piece of land from the Shah over a period of 25 years, at a 20 per cent reduction under the assessed value of the land. The yearly payment amounts to about 25-30 per cent of his income; the peasant—even on Crown lands—paid the owner an average of 50 per cent before land reform. This money is paid into Omran Bank and then loaned back to the farmers through Omran-established cooperatives at 6 per cent interest. Excess funds the Omran Bank invests in projects designed to further the agricultural development of the country.

Dr. Houshang Ram, managing director of Omran Bank, points out another advantage of the Crown lands program. An Iranian village is an integrated economic unit, often including wet farming and dry farming. The Shah gives a village in its entirety to its farmers, permitting the village structure to continue. Under private land reform, however, an owner must be allowed to choose the land he will keep. Not only will he select the best land for himself, but the withdrawal of this land from the village "pool" will tend to disrupt the economic unity of the town.

To cope with the shortage of water in many areas, Omran Bank now is encouraging peasant holders of tiny plots to sell their land to their neighbors, up to a limit of

20 hectares, and always within the same village. Omran then undertakes to find a job for the displaced seller.

All these problems multiply enormously in the realm of public domain lands, partly because these lands tend to be marginal in the first place. Also, there is no organization with single responsibility to follow up the distribution work, as in the case of Omran Bank for Crown lands. Handing out public domain lands is the responsibility of the Ministry of Agriculture, which has myriad other tasks in the country's agricultural development. Hence title clearing and land survey work move extremely slowly in the case of public domain lands.

The Shah's introduction of a land reform bill before the Majlis in 1959 was aimed at curbing the power of Iran's relatively few giant landowners—the so-called "1,000 families"—who consistently have obstructed social reform in the country. From the time the bill came up for debate before the Majlis in October, 1959, the powerful landowners sought to amend the bill to the point of emasculation. They enlisted the support of leading mullahs (Moslem clergymen) who declared that the forced taking of land at arbitrary prices would be "confiscation," opposed by the Koran. The mullahs apparently feared that the land reform bill foreshadowed the seizure of church lands.

This line of attack was so successful that the bill, as finally passed March 15, 1960, does not make it compulsory for a landowner to sell his excess acreage to the government. He may instead sell it to private buyers, with the proviso that half the proceeds be turned over to the Government as a lands development tax. It is far from certain that adequate machinery will be set up to insure that the landlord actually sells his surplus land to a private buyer.

The landowners also were successful in arranging that a vague "fair and just" price should be set for land sales, instead of the arbitrary government figure, which would have been based on ten times the annual produce of a piece of land. Since the government would have established this value on the basis of past tax payments, and since the land owners often paid only a fraction of their due taxes, the price put on their lands would have been far below actual value. Under the bill's amendment on this score the landlords were cleared from having to account for past taxes, yet will receive a fair market value for their lands.

Basic amounts of land allowed to an owner under the bill are 400 hectares of irrigated land and 800 hectares of dry farming land. Successful amendments were introduced allowing an owner to distribute amounts over and above these limits to his heirs, to retain additional lands if he brings them under cultivation, and to keep still other acreage being farmed by mechanization.

By the time the battered bill emerged from the Majlis, Dr. Houshang Ram, the Shah's land reform expert, felt moved to put several questions before the monarch:

1. Has it been estimated how large an area of cultivable land will remain in the entire country after the landlords have set aside for their own use the maximum area they are allowed?

2. Under these conditions, if only a limited number of families receive the left-over lands, will this not add to the already existing dissatisfactions of millions of farmers who are left without land? Add to this the administrative and financial problems that will arise from the transfer of lands and other troubles created during the transfer. What, then, will be the outcome of enforcing this bill?[5]

[5] Quoted by permission of Dr. Houshang Ram, managing director of Omran Bank, Teheran, Iran.

By asking these and other questions Dr. Ram was not trying to add to the burdens of his royal chief, but to warn him of possible new troubles rising from the land reform bill which the Shah's opponents had forced through the Majlis. In effect Dr. Ram was saying that the power of the "1,000 families" would not be crushed by the amended land reform bill, that false hopes raised among the peasantry might turn to despair and disillusionment as the land reform bill failed in application, and that this despair might lead to resentment against the Shah, in whose name the bill had been promulgated.

In all this the United States has a direct interest, since Washington has spent enormous treasure and effort to maintain the stability of the Shah's regime since the mid-1950's. Whatever threatens to undermine the Shah's position threatens to wash out American efforts over the years, as well as to enhance Communist hopes of dominating Iran.

At the individual level consider also the morale of American specialists called in under the United States aid program to advise Iran on irrigation problems, the bringing of new lands under cultivation, operation of village co-operatives, planting of village truck gardens on unused plots, and a host of other matters connected with intelligent land use. Such technicians may spend two years of hard work in Iran, only to leave defeated by an ancient social pattern which they, as American outsiders, have been powerless to attack frontally.

Multiply this story a hundred times throughout the Middle East, throw in diplomatic disputes and rivalries between rulers, and one glimpses the arena in which America's Middle Eastern interests are being served and the kind of problems confronting the men who serve them.

# CHAPTER 7

# Where Do the Soviets Stand?

From the first days of the Iraqi revolution of July 14, 1958, the Soviet Union began a long-term massive effort to plant its influence firmly in Baghdad. Not only was there the opportunity to drive the Communist political wedge deeper into the Middle East; there was also the chance, through trade and aid deals, to siphon off some of Iraq's pounds sterling to help meet Russia's hard currency commitments in the West.

As with Egypt and Syria, so with the Iraqi regime of Abdel Karim Kassem—Moscow dangled the lure of speedy industrialization through low-interest credits advanced without political strings. The bait was snapped up, partly because Iraqi Communists were active in the new regime, but also because Iraqis in general—cut off entirely from the Communist bloc by the former government of Nuri es-Said—had been ready to accept the Soviets at face value as technological supermen who had launched the first sputnik and photographed the back side of the moon before anyone in the West had done so.

It was not long before the bright edges of this image began to tarnish. Early in its relationship with Baghdad, the Soviet Union made the much-publicized gesture of presenting two ambulances to the Red Crescent Society in Baghdad. Though manufactured in the Soviet Union, the ambulances turned out to be exact copies of an old model Pontiac, down to the plastic headdress on the Indian figurehead. This similarity was not lost on Iraqis, long accustomed to Western cars.

Soon a steady stream of Soviet trucks began to enter Baghdad under the terms of the Soviet aid agreement with Iraq. Here again disillusionment set in. To Iraqi drivers the Soviet vehicles looked suspiciously like copies of American models turned out in the 1940's. The trucks ran and did their job, but they scarcely enhanced Soviet prestige among the Iraqis.

Baghdad taxi drivers were another element soon disaffected by the Iraqi government's efforts to redirect Iraqi trade toward the Eastern bloc. Though the taxi drivers were vocal supporters of the regime's anti-imperialist line flaunted by the regime, they were at the same time devoted to Chevrolet taxis. When the government forbade the import of American cars and tried to force Communist models on the drivers, they protested vigorously.

The taxi drivers had another very human reason for disliking the Russians. Underpaid Soviet technicians refused to pay the full fare for a taxi ride, amounting as it did to about one-fifth of their total per diem allowance. Soon Iraqi taxi drivers began looking the other way when they spotted a Russian at the curb.

There was good cause for the Russians' stinginess, though the drivers may not have known it. The Iraqi government was paying the salaries of Communist specialists directly to their embassies or home governments. The Soviet Embassy in Baghdad, for example, collected its citizens' salaries, then doled out about four dollars per day to each technician, promising him the rest when he returned to Russia. Presumably this was done to guard against defections.

Soviet engineers and other instructors sent to Baghdad found the language barrier an almost insurmountable block between themselves and Iraqis. Soviet doctors invited to lecture to Iraqi medical students found themselves aided by interpreters who understood Russian but had no specialized knowledge of medical terms. By the time the Soviets' remarks were filtered through the interpreters, the lecture was medically meaningless.

In other cases Soviet technical personnel, trying to explain the operation of a complex piece of machinery, were forced to explain to a Russian interpreter, who turned the instruction from Russian into English. An Iraqi interpreter then translated the English into Arabic for the Iraqi students. Shades of technical meaning often were lost in the process.

All these fringe irritations taken together do not necessarily mean that Soviet-Iraqi economic collaboration is going to fail. The program barely has swung into motion and it would be dangerous to predict what its final results may be. But the early signs have been of small comfort to Iraqi authorities, who in the first flush of their revolution had disbanded the old Western-aided Iraq Development Board and scrapped the elaborate plans for the country's development which that board had drawn up.

Founded by the Iraqi government, the development board had had at its command 70 per cent of Iraq's substantial income from oil. Over a period of years this board aimed at transforming the Iraqi economy through a series of irrigation, hydroelectric, flood control, road- and rail-building, and other agricultural and industrial development projects. The Iraqi government goal, enthusiastically endorsed by Britain and the United States, was to lift the depressed living standards of the people sufficiently fast to stem the revolutionary tide then sweeping the Arab Middle East.

Iraq was to become the shining example of an Arab land able to meet its people's needs because of—or perhaps despite—its firm allegiance to the West. So sanguine were Western planners that Lord Salter, in a report drawn up at the request of the Iraqi government in 1955, declared: "Granting wise administration, peace and stability, Iraq now has a prospect of a rapid advance in national prosperity and individual welfare which has been rarely equalled in history."[1]

But the Iraqi government during this period was dominated by a tight oligarchy of wealthy landowning families and tribal sheiks, at the apex of which stood Premier Nuri es-Said as the ultimate expression of the oligarchy's power. It was Nuri's task to steer a course which would transform Iraq's feudal economy quickly enough to mollify the masses without at the same time alienating the ruling class. The result was the concentration of the development board's activities on massive flood control, irrigation, and communications projects which—though they finally would have helped the downtrodden peasant—along the way appeared to benefit the great landlords first.

The outcome is history. Swept away by the Iraqi revolution of July, 1958, was the power of the ruling oligarchy

[1] *The Development of Iraq* (London: Caxton, for Iraq Development Board, 1955), p. 123, as quoted by *The Middle East: A Political and Economic Survey* (London: Oxford University Press, 1958), p. 257.

and all for which it stood, including the Iraq Development Board. Brutally slain on the day of the revolution were young King Feisal, his uncle Abdul Ilah, and Nuri himself, who was shot down and dragged through the streets while disguised as a woman, trying to escape the mob's fury. Clearly the Iraq Development Board's long-range plans for transforming the country had not weighed against the people's anger at the feudal character and persistent pro-Westernism of Nuri es-Said's iron rule.

In this mood of angry republicanism Premier Kassem's government, already penetrated by seasoned Communist agitators, figuratively tore up the development board's plans, abolished the organization itself, and divided its functions among several ministries. The slate, now wiped clean, would be rewritten with a new development program aimed at the people themselves. Indeed, in a speech to the Iraqi people in April, 1960, General Kassem promised that within seven years Iraq would enjoy the highest standard of living in the world, and would be sending out a steady flow of Iraqi technicians to aid "backward" nations of the world.

Even as it scrapped the old plans, however, the Iraqi government began to discover that it had nothing with which to replace them. The knowledge seeped home that never had Iraq had a technical planning staff of its own. To be sure, the development board had been staffed largely by Iraqis, though one British and one American member had sat on the board with full voting rights. But the projects themselves had been tendered out to American, British, West German, and other Western firms to survey and build. Thus the blueprints had been drawn to specifications which Iraqi engineers could not decipher, even had they wanted to.

Nor did the problem end here. In its zeal to clean house General Kassem's government has dismissed or allowed to retire at least 4,000 of the government's 20,000 civil servants, chiefly at the upper levels. For example, the entire staff of the development board's Contract Legal Affairs office, responsible for administering about 350 contracts with foreign firms, was let go. Sixty per cent of directors general of government departments lost their jobs. The result was administrative chaos, only partly reduced to this day despite the government's rehiring of some dismissed persons.

Accompanying this purge was the passage of new labor laws designed to please the working class, but in practice so restrictive that many foreign firms packed up and left rather than get entangled in endless red tape should they wish to release unessential workers. In other cases contracts were unilaterally abrogated by the Iraqi government and the firms concerned have not yet been able to collect from the government for past payments due.

One American company, the Tibbett, Abbott, McCarthy and Stratton general contracting firm, had its properties seized by the Iraqi government in March, 1959, and more than a year later still had had neither explanation nor compensation offered by the government. Individual Westerners hired by the defunct development board have been forced to spend a minimum of five weeks in Baghdad, at their own expense, before being granted exit visas and paid even a fraction of their just claims.

Debts owed by the Iraqi government to foreign firms and individuals amount to at least $30,000,000, or about one tenth of a normal year's governmental budget. Payment of these debts, even over a period of time, would be a major budgetary item. Yet until the debts are paid the character rating of Premier Kassem's government will remain zero.

By the spring of 1960 the situation was so bad that the Iraqi government was seeking bids on contracts for road construction and the building of three hospitals—and had not received a single bid. Incredible as it sounds, Iraq, a country with an assured income from oil, had a credit rating so poor that almost no Western firm cared to do business with it.

In part this tragedy had come about through excessive zeal to do away with everything connoting the "imperialist" past; in part it was due to the attempt of Communist Iraqis to shift their country's trade channels from the West toward the East. Prime mover in this attempt had been Minister of Economy Ibrahim Kubbeh, who became the Communists' foremost spokesman in government during the revolution's early days.

By instituting a system of strict import licensing, Kubbeh hoped to force Iraqi merchants and importers to buy only from the Soviet bloc, but because of the public's boycott of inferior Communist goods he was dismissed from his job and given the twin titles of Minister of Agrarian Reform and Acting Minister of Oil. Undaunted, Kubbeh sought in his new jobs to make the Soviet Union Iraq's only supplier of agricultural equipment. Finally an Iraqi dealer in Western farm machinery got a letter through to Premier Kassem, asking why his Minister of Agrarian Reform was buying Russian equipment when Iraqi dealers had heavy inventories of tried and true Western tractors, plows, harrows, and other machinery already in stock. Within ten days of the complaint, in February, 1960, Kubbeh was sacked from both new jobs and, except for some goods still on the restricted list for currency control reasons,

Iraqi merchants were given freedom to buy where they pleased.

By this time the Iraqi economy was in extremely serious straits. Unemployment had crept up steadily as the country's development program shrank. Landowners, fearful of losing their lands under the agrarian reform program, had planted only part of their fields, with the result that the 1959 crops were perhaps 50 per cent of normal. Though plantings improved slightly the next year, drought kept the 1960 crops down to about the same level. Faced with the threat of street riots and looted shops, merchants hesitated to restock their depleted shelves. As a consequence prices moved upward in search of scarce goods.

Even where the Iraqi government was able to generate some forward movement, technical inefficiency often sapped the vitality of the work. To provide power for its new model village of Latafiyah, about thirty miles south of Baghdad, General Kassem's regime had bought two generators from a British firm. Under the deal the British agreed to maintain the generators for nine months after their installation and to train Iraqis to service them after that.

The generators were installed in April, 1959, and the village was formally inaugurated by General Kassem in July. All went well until the British turned the generators over to the Iraqis at the end of the year. Three months later, in April, 1960, a distraught Iraqi entered the British firm's office in Baghdad. "You've got to help us!" the Iraqi cried. "Tomorrow Mikoyan is visiting Latafiyah and we're having trouble with the generators." (Soviet Deputy Premier Anastas I. Mikoyan was in the midst of an eight-day visit to Iraq.)

Out at the village the British discovered to their shock

that not only had the generators been run constantly at full capacity for more than three months, but not once had there been any attempt to service them. Not a single adjustment or check had been made of the generators, though the Iraqis had been told what would happen if the machines were not maintained.

By putting in eight hours of work the British managed to get one generator running so the village would have electric light during Mr. Mikoyan's visit. The other machine required a major overhaul. This the British refused to do, despite the pleas of Iraqi engineers, unless a work order was received from the appropriate government ministry. "We will donate the eight hours of work on the first generator," the British contractor said in effect. "But the overhaul of the second will take time and money, and the government will have to pay for it."

An early act of the revolutionary regime was to sequester the funds and property of Mansour race track. A private club located outside Baghdad, it was synonymous with royalty and privilege. The club owned an intricate new tote board to tabulate bets. Bought at a cost of $3,000,000, the tote board's electronic mechanism was maintained at constant temperature by air conditioning. Learning of the sequestration, race track authorities in Beirut, Lebanon, offered to buy the tote board from the Mansour club.

Club officials went to sequestration officials in Baghdad and requested permission to make the sale, explaining that the proceeds would go into the club's sequestered bank account, merely changing the form of the club's seized assets. The officials refused, the tote board remains unserviced, and soon will be almost worthless. Had the government wished, the proceeds from the sale—amounting, perhaps, to $2,000,000—could have been put to Iraqi government use.

Among the club's sequestered property were two trucks and two passenger cars, one of the latter brand new. The new car was put into a garage. The other vehicles were left outdoors on the concrete. Today they have sunk to their rims on deflated tires, their windows are broken, and parts have been stolen. Throughout the countryside can be seen heavy construction equipment, similarly immobilized and stripped while waiting as long as eighteen months for spare parts replacement.

During this period of confusion, only the Iraq Petroleum Company, Iraq's goose with the golden eggs, continued to expand its production. By the end of 1961 I.P.C. hopes to double its output over the figure which had been achieved at the time of the revolution. In this process I.P.C. receives utmost encouragement from General Kassem's regime, for even the Communists have no desire to tamper with Iraq's major source of income. Though the expansion would assure an increased income from oil, it could not by itself restore the government's ruined credit and character rating which had robbed Baghdad of managerial and technical skills.

No hint of these economic problems was allowed to leak out through government channels, though in fact the Iraqi consumer could feel in his pocketbook what was happening. Stoutly the administration, from Premier Kassem down, continued to insist that great forward strides were being made and that unequalled prosperity lay just around the corner. A pamphlet handed me in Baghdad by the Ministry of National Guidance in April, 1960, affirmed: "From the early days of the Revolution, grand victories and substantial gains were achieved in the economic, political and cultural fields. Housing schemes, land reform and the building of factories is being carried on."

At the time that pamphlet was written, the building of factories remained almost entirely on paper, while land reform had succeeded primarily in reducing crop production in Iraq. The pamphlet was correct in saying that some housing was being built, perhaps as much as any new government could have achieved in the time.

At least verbally Premier Kassem's government had a new development program to supplant the old, for on Dec. 3, 1959, the Premier had announced an "interim" Four Year Plan, involving the expenditure of 400,000,000 Iraqi dinars, or about $1,120,000,000. Iraqi economists, charged with translating the General's totally unrealistic words into action, concocted a "plan" which appeared to include some projects already built and paid for by the old regime. Some schemes mentioned were sheer pie in the sky, while still others called for the building of factories which had been specified in the Soviet-Iraqi aid agreement signed in Moscow in March, 1959. Thus attention was drawn to the extension of Soviet credits as the chief vehicle for the Iraqi republic's anticipated economic progress.

The Soviet aid agreement, offering credits up to 550,000,000 rubles (about $140,000,000), had been engineered on the Iraqi side by Mr. Kubbeh, at that time still Minister of Economy. Upon examination the Soviets appeared to have picked and chosen among Iraq's many development needs those projects which Russian technicians were best able to handle. Thus the hastily conceived aid program did not, by Western standards at least, promise a well constructed attack on Iraq's basic needs.

The aid agreement divided visibly into two parts, one calling for the construction of twenty-six factories, for which the Soviets would select sites, construct buildings, provide machinery, and staff with trained Iraqis. The second part of the aid program promised Soviet technical assistance and design work in such realms as flood control and irrigation works, conversion of the Baghdad-Basra railroad to standard gauge, and a geological survey of Iraq.

Iraq had begun buying major quantities of Soviet arms even before the economic aid agreement was signed. While no outsider knows for certain, Western diplomatic observers believe Iraq is paying for these weapons under some kind of separate arrangement. By early summer of 1960 Iraq was known to have substantial numbers of Soviet tanks and artillery pieces, as well as jet fighters and bombers and motor torpedo boats.

In a giant military parade in Baghdad on July 14, 1959, I saw eighty T-54 Russian tanks and forty-five smaller T-34 models roll by, together with 152 mm. gun howitzers, 100 mm. antiaircraft guns, 132 mm. rockets, 120 mm. mortars, and other types of Soviet artillery. Nine months later Iraq was believed by Western military experts to have approximately 30 MIG jet fighters, some of them late model MIG-17D's, plus an unknown number of IL-28 jet bombers.

The ability of the Iraqi armed forces to assimilate this equipment quickly is open to question. From 1954 until the revolution the United States Military Assistance and Advisory Group had made little progress in persuading the Iraqi Army to set up an efficient warehousing and supply system. No one officer or department within the Iraqi Army ever knew at one time what equipment and munitions the army's supply dumps held. On occasion the Iraqi Army bought ammunition, only to discover later that it had been adequately stocked in that line.

As a result of this administrative looseness, the Iraqi Army at best could have sent only one division across the desert to fight in Syria or Jordan, and could have sustained that unit no more than a week or ten days, in the view of Western military experts. Prior to the revolution the Iraqi Army had been supplied with about equal amounts of British and American equipment. For some time, at least, the addition of large quantities of Soviet matériel to this armament would tend to confuse further the training and supply problem. There is no reason to believe Soviet military advisers have been any more successful than their American and British predecessors in tightening up the army's indispensable rear echelon commands.

Thus in all probability Soviet arms have not yet transformed the Iraqi Army into a disciplined offensive weapon with which to thrust at its neighbors, though its potential firepower certainly has been increased. This does not mean that the Soviet military program in Iraq is mere propaganda, since progressively the Iraqis are being forced to depend upon the Soviets for replacement, spare parts, ammunition, and training.

The Soviets at the time of their aid deal with Iraq appeared to be in a prime position to cash in on the anti-Western feeling and economic turmoil prevailing in Iraq. By early summer of 1960—more than one year after the signing of the agreement in Moscow—they had not so cashed in. Emotional antipathy against the West did not, for many Iraqis, include rejection of the Western cars, farm equipment, and construction machinery with which these Iraqis earned their bread and butter.

Had the Soviets been able to offer goods of comparable quality, they might have been accepted. But clearly Soviet products did not measure up to the standards to which

Iraqis were used. Thus Mr. Kubbeh's efforts to freeze out Western imports in favor of Communist goods soured the atmosphere of the Soviet aid agreement at the beginning. To this was added the developing friction between individual Iraqis and Soviets deriving from cultural and religious differences and the language barrier. In short, Iraqi xenophobism began to transfer itself from the vanished Westerners to the new foreigners on the scene.

At a time when General Kassem urgently needed concrete achievements at which to point, Soviet help had failed to materialize in a form that could be looked at, touched, and measured, except for weapons of war and for individual pieces of civilian equipment generally inferior to comparable Western models. As late as June, 1960, ground had not been broken for a single one of the twenty-six factories described in the Soviet aid agreement of March, 1959. Sites had been selected for some of them and "soil testing" had been carried out. But this was hardly enough to satisfy impatient Iraqis.

On February 14, 1960, Soviet experts had begun survey work on conversion of the Baghdad-Basra railway from meter to standard gauge. Meanwhile, the railway administration had suffered so badly from the firing of personnel after the revolution and their replacement by poorly-trained pro-Communists, that the system literally was grinding to a halt. In part the Soviet advisers were blamed by the Iraqi public for what was happening to the country's railroads.

The sole civilian project for which the Soviets could justly claim credit for prompt delivery was the supplying of four 1,000-watt transmitters to the Iraqi broadcasting system. Many Iraqis recalled that this government-owned radio system had been Communist-dominated from the beginning of the revolution.

Having swung so far away from the West, the pendulum now began to swing back. Iraqi merchants and even some government officials hinted openly to the United States Embassy that American trade centers should be opened in Iraq. In 1959, as in every previous year at least back to 1956, Britain, the United States, and West Germany had ranked one, two, three among nations in the sale of goods to Iraq. Taken as a bloc the Communist nations had moved up from twelfth place in sales to Iraq in 1958 to fifth place in 1959. But this had been accomplished during the first flush of enthusiasm after the revolution, before the general inferiority of Communist goods had become a matter of comment.

Hidden within Iraq's new commercial agencies law was additional evidence that the Iraqi government had not forgotten the importance of its trade ties with the West. Promulgated in February, 1960, the law stipulated that in the future all companies operating in Iraq must be at least 51 per cent owned by resident Iraqi capital. This stipulation was aimed chiefly at breaking the long-standing British monopoly in some fields of Iraqi business.

Exempted from the law, however, were foreign companies engaged in exporting Iraqi products. At first even Iraqi bankers and businessmen were puzzled by this, since the only apparent foreign exporter of an Iraqi product was the Iraq Petroleum Company, whose operations lay outside the commercial agencies law. Then it was recalled that one other foreign company exported an Iraqi product—an American-owned firm named MacAndrews & Forbes, whose sale of Iraq's licorice root amounted to the country's third largest export item. Clearly, in formulating its apparently anti-Western law, the Iraqi Government had taken care not to disturb this export facility.

In the field of education also, the Iraqi government was beginning to show preference for Western over Communist teachers; this despite the fact the Ministry of Education remained heavily infiltrated by Communists. In the spring of 1960 Iraq advertised for 200 foreign teachers at the high school and university levels. Two requirements were listed—academic experience and ability to teach in English. Thus, though the offers were open to almost all national- ities, the scales were weighted in favor of Americans and Britons. Privately the anti-Communist Minister of Educa- tion let it be known that he hoped for a preponderance of teachers from the West. He could not say so publicly, since his own ministry was a Communist stronghold.

By the spring of 1960 American Embassy officials in Baghdad were cautioning against too swift an upsurge of Western confidence about Iraq. Quite possibly a number of the invisible factories described in the Soviet aid agree- ment were in the process of preassembly and testing in the Soviet Union, prior to shipment to Iraq in prefabricated form. American officers pointed to the impressive indus- trial exhibition, including a permanent cinema, which the Soviets had opened in Baghdad in April, 1960. A few weeks before that exhibition opened, the fair grounds had been bare. One day the entire exhibition, including theater, arrived crated on shipboard at Basra, was given priority transport to Baghdad and put up at lightning speed. The same could happen with the promised factories, causing some of the current Iraqi chilliness toward the Soviets to disappear.

Nonetheless, as 1960 edged into summer it seeemed clear that the West had a better than even chance to continue its dominance in the Iraqi trading market, with the possibility later on of moving back into the economic aid field. Obviously the Iraqi armed forces would continue to remain dependent on the Soviet Union unless and until a truly anti-Communist government of Iraq decided to cut its losses on the Communist equipment already acquired.

The Iraqi government possessed an ace in the hole should it ever want to break away entirely from the Soviet bloc. This was its income from oil, produced by a Western-owned firm and sold to Europe for hard currency. In 1959 Iraq had earned $258,000,000 from oil and this figure was expected to rise to about $275,000,000 in 1960. Of this amount 50 per cent was available for the country's development program, instead of the 70 per cent of oil income earmarked for development by the Nuri es-Said regime.

In other words, the Communist bloc had not become a market for Iraq's leading money earner. The country's major income continued to come from the West, despite Baghdad's involvement with the Communists in the aid field. This income from oil was so substantial that at any time Iraq could liquidate most of its commitments with the Eastern bloc, though it might continue to maintain the small amounts of Communist trade which even the old regime had allowed.

The story of Soviet penetration of Egypt and Syria was markedly different. Since 1955 this penetration has been spectacular both in an absolute and relative sense. The very size and suddenness of the Soviet aid programs to Cairo and Damascus made them appear to have sprung out of a vacuum. From Moscow's point of view such was not the case. To Soviet leaders their economic and military aid endeavors in Egypt and Syria, as well as in Afghanistan, Yemen, and later in Iraq, represented the latest and most successful step in a long-standing Russian attempt to gain a foothold in the Middle East.

In the days of the czars these efforts had been frustrated by British and French control of the area. For some years after the Bolshevik revolution in 1917 the Soviet Union's new leaders were too preoccupied with the consolidation of their internal power to have energy left over for expansion in the Middle East. Only in the late thirties did the southward push begin again, aimed at the traditional targets of Turkey and Iran.

Stalin tried immediately after World War II to exploit war weariness and unrest in Greece and Turkey and to establish a Soviet-backed regime in northwestern Iran (Azerbaijan). Blocked in Greece and Turkey by President Truman's containment policy and in Iran by pressure from the United Nations to withdraw his forces, Stalin virtually abandoned expansionist aims in the Middle East.

Shortly after Stalin's death, renewed Soviet interest in the area was heralded by the extension of a modest line of credit ($3,500,000) to Afghanistan. This was the beginning of an intervention which soon focused on Egypt and Syria. The choice of these countries was not accidental. Both Syrian and Egyptian leaders resented the West's attempt to impose the Baghdad Pact upon them and the adherence of Iraq to that alliance. Arab thinking also identified the United States and Britain with the creation of Israel. Finally, in 1955 President Nasser had been unable to obtain Western arms to counter what he regarded as an intensified Israeli threat to Egypt.

The first fruits of these conditions, from the Soviet point of view, was the conclusion in September, 1955, of a deal committing Cairo to the purchase of an estimated

$200,000,000 worth of Communist arms. At somewhat the same time, though the agreement never was publicized as it had been in Egypt, Syria began to receive shipments of Soviet weapons. Here the Soviet entry had been smoothed by consolidation of Syrian political power in the hands of radical young Syrian Socialists and Army officers who looked upon the West as Syria's enemy. In both Syria and Egypt the arms sales were followed by the extension of Soviet economic credits and a sharp rise in trade between these Arab countries and the Communist bloc.

Though offered by the Soviets as components of an integrated package, trade on the one hand and economic and technical assistance on the other in fact were separate items. Until 1954 trade between the Middle East and the Communist bloc had been relatively unimportant for both sides. In 1938, for example, the Middle East obtained 5 per cent of its imports and sold 3 per cent of its exports to the Soviet Union, though Arab trade with other countries of Eastern Europe was somewhat higher.[2] These trade levels remained static, and in some cases even declined, through 1953.

The following year, marking the start of the Soviet breakthrough in the Middle East, saw Egyptian and Syrian trade with the Communist bloc begin to rise. In 1959 the Soviet Union, Communist China, East Germany, and Czechoslovakia were Egypt's best customers in that order, with cotton the principal export concerned. The Soviets alone bought 26,829,137 Egyptian pounds worth of Egyptian cotton (about $75,000,000) during the first nine months of 1959, more than West Germany, Italy, India,

[2] Robert Loring Allen, *Middle Eastern Economic Relations with the Soviet Union, Eastern Europe, and Mainland China* (Charlottesville, Va.: University of Virginia Press, 1958), p. 14.

Japan, the Sudan, Britain, and the United States put together.

From 1954 through 1958 Communist bloc purchases of Syrian goods, primarily raw cotton, shot up almost fortyfold. However, Syria consistently bought more from the West during these years than it did from the East. This fact, coupled with growing political coolness between Moscow and the United Arab Republic, caused a slump in Sino-Soviet bloc imports of Syrian products in 1959.

The totals of Soviet economic and technical aid credits to Egypt and Syria are equally impressive in their growth. In October, 1957, Syria had received from the Soviet Union a line of credit worth $168,000,000 to finance the foreign currency costs of nineteen development projects. The terms of repayment are worth noting because they set the general pattern of later Soviet credit extensions to the Arab world.

Credits offered to Syria could be drawn over a period of seven years and would be repaid at 2.5 per cent interest per year, calculated on each part of the credit from the date it was drawn. Payment for each portion of the credit would begin only after the project concerned was in operation, and would be repaid in twelve annual installments.

This arrangement was followed in January, 1958, by the signing of a similar agreement offering Soviet credits worth $175,000,000 to Egypt, to cover forty specific development projects and possibly twenty-five more. Terms of repayment were patterned closely on the Syrian model. From Egypt's standpoint these credits formed part of a massive five-year industralization program scheduled to cost $750,000,000.

The building of Egypt's High Aswan Dam lay outside the scope of the $750,000,000 industrialization program.

Through its construction of the world's largest dam at Aswan on the River Nile, Egypt hopes to reclaim possibly 2,000,000 acres of presently uncultivable desert land and to irrigate year round a further 700,000 acres now watered only in flood time. The dam also is scheduled to produce up to ten billion kilowatt hours of electricity a year. Completion of the dam, according to the Egyptian Ministry of Public Works, will increase Egypt's agricultural income by 35 per cent.

Until 1956 President Nasser, as well as the United States and Britain, apparently had hoped the dam would remain entirely a Western preserve, so far as foreign currency costs were concerned. Of these foreign exchange components, estimated at $400,000,000, the World Bank had offered a $200,000,000 loan, to be supplemented by a further $70,000,000 from the United States and British governments. It seemed likely the remaining $130,000,000 also would be forthcoming.

This reckoned without Mr. Nasser's plunge into a military relationship with the Soviet Union and Secretary of State Dulles' consequent abrupt withdrawal of the American offer to finance the dam. For a time the whole project hung fire, obscured by Egypt's nationalization of the Suez Canal Company and the invasion of Egypt by Israel, Britain, and France in the fall of 1956.

In December, 1958, the project came back into focus when Egypt accepted a Soviet loan of $100,000,000 to finance the first stage of the High Dam. The Russians stipulated that Soviet technicians and machinery must be used in the construction. At that time the U.A.R. government announced its freedom from commitments for the second and far more expensive stage of the dam, implying that Western governments would be welcome to bid on the project.

But this possibility was ruled out in January, 1960, when Cairo announced its acceptance of a Russian offer to build the second stage of the dam on the same basis as the first—namely, using Soviet men and equipment. The amount of credit advanced in this new transaction was said to be 100,000,000 Egyptian pounds, or more than $280,000,000. Soviet help would enable the dam to be completed in 1967, three years earlier than originally planned, according to the U.A.R. government, and at the reduced total cost of 337,000,000 Egyptian pounds, or about $968,000,000.

When all Sino-Soviet bloc credits to the U.A.R. are lumped together—for Czechoslovakia, East Germany, and Communist China had joined with Russia in tendering credits—totals through the spring of 1960 were as follows:

Egypt had received $315,000,000 worth of credits to purchase arms and all of it had been used. It also appeared that Egypt had totally repaid this loan. In addition Egypt had received economic credit commitments totalling $596,000,000, of which about $56,000,000 worth is known to have been drawn. Syria had used up its total of $128,-000,000 in military credits and had been promised $195,000,-000 worth of economic aid credits, of which an estimated $70,000,000 had been drawn.

To service projects implemented under these credit agreements Egypt had 655 Communist technicians on its territory during 1959, according to figures disclosed by American authorities in Washington. During the same year the Syrian region of the U.A.R. allowed in 735 Communist technicians, an increase of 460 over 1958.

Statistically, therefore, the Communist bloc was far more deeply engaged militarily and economically in the

U.A.R. than it was in Iraq, despite the fact the Iraqi government was more friendly to Moscow than was President Nasser. Taken by themselves, however, the statistics could be misleading, for hidden among them were factors both favorable and unfavorable from the Western point of view.

Note already has been made of Egyptian and Syrian displeasure at certain Communist trading practices, notably the resale of Egyptian and Syrian cotton at discounts on the Western European market. Another Soviet bloc trick has been to stay out of the U.A.R. cotton buying market until Western buyers have made their entry.

Then the Communists descend upon the market, buy heavily, and force prices up beyond the level Western purchasers wish to pay. This serves the Communist end of keeping Western purchases low and ensuring the U.A.R.'s continued economic dependence on the Soviet bloc. For the Soviets to do this is easy, since each year Egypt and Syria commit substantial amounts of their cotton to pay for their imports of Communist goods. The Communists merely wait until the time is ripe to pick up these commitments.

Also annoying to the U.A.R. government is the Soviet habit of delivering goods long after Egypt and Syria have paid for them with their commodities. This puts Cairo and Damascus in the position of creditors to the bloc, left without the promised goods or cash to put to work. These trading practices are made possible by the bilateral trade agreements under which almost all U.A.R.-Communist trade is carried on. A typical barter deal, for example, calls for the commitment of a certain amount of Egyptian cotton in return for Czechoslovak manufactures, or Russian crude oil, or Soviet tanks.

Thus each deal is withdrawn from the give and take of the open market, permitting the Communists to place artificially high price tags on their goods, and even on occasion to make substitutions in their deliveries. So long as Egypt is unable to sell her cotton to the free world, she is almost helpless to escape this kind of arrangement. The same holds true for Syria in trying to dispose of her cotton and other agricultural products.

Ostensibly its trade with the Soviet bloc is beneficial to the U.A.R., since both Egypt and Syria maintain trade surpluses with Communist countries. To some extent this trade is genuinely helpful to Cairo and Damascus in providing goods and services which otherwise would have to be paid for in hard cash. At the same time the U.A.R.'s need to dispose of its cotton forces its continued dependence on the Sino-Soviet bloc, and the conditions of this trade make Egyptians and Syrians increasingly restive. An examination of the separate economies of the two regions of the U.A.R. points up the nation's dilemma.

To understand Egypt's difficulty one must go back to 1954. At that time, prior to Cairo's arms deal with the Soviets, Egypt sold two thirds of its cotton to Western Europe alone. Additional sales to the United States and Canada, to the Arab world and the Far East, built up the total to 75 per cent of the entire crop. Since that time, however, the world cotton market has experienced a general slump, and cotton-producing countries have been left with large surpluses.

For Egypt this problem was exacerbated by the free world's rejection of her cotton following Cairo's purchase of arms from the Soviets. Today Egypt's former Western customers have found new sources for their cotton, and

Egyptian growers would find it extremely difficult to re-enter the Western market.

Today Britain, formerly Egypt's chief buyer, buys most of its cotton from the friendly Sudan. Yet the Sudan still is left with a yearly surplus. The United States has so great a surplus of cotton that the United States government subsidizes cotton exports to help American farmers get rid of their crops. As a result of this surplus Canada, for example, finds it cheaper and far more dependable to buy American cotton than Egyptian. The only way in which the United States could buy substantial amounts of Egyptian cotton would be to hold its purchases off the world market, since their resale would only depress the market and add to the United States' own surpluses.

All these factors taken together produced a radical change in Egypt's cotton selling pattern. According to the National Bank of Egypt, 63.4 per cent of Egypt's cotton exports went to the Communist bloc during the season from September 1, 1957 through August 30, 1958. (Egypt's marketing season opens on September 1 each year.) The following year this percentage rose to 64.2 per cent. Roughly the same percentage prevails this year.

Following the recent improvement in relations between the U.A.R. and the West, there has been a slight increase in Western purchases of Egyptian growths. Western Europe bought 25 per cent of the Egyptian crop during the marketing year ending August 30, 1959, compared with 20.2 per cent the year before. As a measure of its interest in the U.A.R.'s economic betterment, the United States planned to buy $8,000,000 to $10,000,000 worth of Egyptian cotton during the 1959-1960 selling season, or about 80 per cent of America's cotton import quota for the year. These improvements, welcome as they were to Cairo, did not herald anything like a swing back to Egypt's traditional Western markets.

All during this period Egypt continued to buy American and Western European machinery for its vast industrialization program. For this machinery it had to pay hard cash. Yet Egypt was buying from the West far more than it sold. The only alternative was to dip into its reserves of gold and foreign exchange to pay for its imports of Western machine goods.

International Monetary Fund figures showed that gold and foreign exchange held by the National Bank of Egypt stood at $957,000,000 in 1951. By December of 1959 this figure had dropped to 74.5 million Egyptian pounds, or $214,560,000 at the official rate of $2.88 to the pound. In fact, the bulk of Cairo's commercial transactions with the West are conducted through the export pound, 17.6 per cent cheaper than the official pound. Thus even $214,-560,000 worth of reserves is an inflated figure.

This drop in Egypt's gold and foreign exchange reserves from nearly one billion dollars in 1951 to $214,-560,000 at the end of 1959 is a partial measure of the trade deficit Egypt has been running with the West. The full deficit is even larger, for Suez Canal revenues, income from tourism and other sources have been poured in to keep the deficit from increasing.

In 1959 some Western economists estimated that if Egypt paid all its known debts to the United States, Italy, Canada, and West Germany, plus its estimated debts to other Western lands, Cairo would wipe out all its gold and foreign exchange reserves and then some. This estimate allowed for the fact that Egypt has a creditor status of about 60,000,000 Egyptian pounds, representing Egyptian goods delivered but not paid for.

Egypt also has 38,500,000 of uncommitted pounds sterling, accruing from the Anglo-Egyptian financial settlement of February, 1959. President Nasser intends to hang onto this liquid asset to keep Egypt's five-year industrialization program pump primed, should Soviet financing cease.

Even when Suez Canal revenues and all other income is figured in, Egypt's foreign trade deficit amounts to about $60,000,000. To wipe out or even reduce this yearly drain Cairo has two alternatives—either stop buying Western goods or find some way of selling more of its own products to the free world. The crux of the matter is cotton, Egypt's major money earner. So long as Cairo sells most of its cotton to Communist countries, the Soviet bloc's virtual stranglehold over Egypt's economy will be continued.

In the realm of military aid Egypt also is basically committed to the Soviets. Whereas Iraq's army to date has shifted only partially from Western to Communist equipment, the armed forces of Egypt and Syria have made virtually total conversion to Soviet weapons. Despite the U.A.R.'s claim that it can manufacture ammunition and spare parts for many of these items, obviously it cannot make heavy tanks, MIG fighters, or submarines.

From the standpoint of Communist influence in the U.A.R., Moscow's building of the High Aswan Dam may prove to be less meaningful than its military aid and cotton purchases, despite the fact that the dam is scheduled to become mankind's greatest single engineering project. Certainly Cairo's awarding of the dam to Moscow means the Soviet Union will occupy a central place in the U.A.R.'s chief development plans over the next seven years. This represents a triumph for the Soviets, but the triumph has certain qualifications.

Moscow has committed its technical aid prestige to a long haul of at least seven years at a time when political relations between Cairo and the Soviet Union are somewhat strained. No matter how much relations between Mr. Nasser and the West may improve, Moscow will be constrained to finish its project efficiently, or face the charge of inability to build the dam.

Also, awarding the second stage of the dam to the Soviets probably was a practical rather than an anti-Western gesture on the part of President Nasser. There is validity in the Soviet argument that the first and second stages of the dam to some extent overlap and that it will be cheaper for the U.A.R. to have one set of engineers carry through the entire project. Already Soviet engineers have reduced the cost of the dam's first stage by substituting seven open diversion channels for the underground tunnels which Western engineers originally had planned.

In some ways the situation of Syria is strikingly similar to that of Egypt in its relationship to the Communist bloc. From one point of view Mr. Nasser merely doubled his dependence upon the Soviets when he accepted the merger of Syria and Egypt under Cairo's rule. Syrian merchants persist in buying Western goods, thus running up a trade deficit for their country. Only the Soviet bloc is willing to buy substantial amounts of Syrian cotton and other farm products. And the Syrian Army, or First Army of the United Arab Republic, uses Soviet weapons.

Syria's chief foreign trade problem is its preference for Western goods and its inability to pay for these goods through exports to the Western world. Thus Syria's imbalance of trade with the free world is chronic and heavy. During the first three quarters of 1959, West Germany, France, Britain, and the United States in that order were at the top of the list among nations selling goods to Syria. The Soviet Union, leader among Communist nations, placed twelfth on the list. Though Western powers tend to swap rungs on the ladder in trade with Syria, they are consistently at the top.

This situation contributes to Syria's perennial foreign trade gap, running roughly at the rate of $57,000,000 yearly. Even to keep its annual deficit at this level, Syria must have good crop years, since its principal exports are cotton, barley, wheat, tobacco, vegetables, and fruits. The direct relationship between the weather and Syrian exports was shown up dramatically in 1958, 1959, and 1960, when severe droughts dried up Syria's grain exports and caused the northern region of the U.A.R. to import cereals, including surplus wheat under the United States Public Law 480 program.

Syria has three other sources of income—revenue from transit trade crossing from Lebanon into the interior of the Arab world and vice versa; oil pipelines crossing Syrian territory; and money sent home from abroad by Syrian citizens living outside the country.

Each year the Syrian government's official books show revenue from these sources to have closed the trade gap and given Syria a balanced import-export flow. Western observers must accept these figures—since there are no others on which to go—though Syrian economists themselves admit there is no standardized procedure by which this bookkeeping balance is reached.

In recent months Syria has had more success than Egypt in reducing its economic dependence on the Soviets. Primarily this is due to the comparatively wider range of farm products which Syria has to sell. The Communist nations themselves have sharply lowered their purchases of

Syrian goods, while Syrian sales to the West have gone up a degree.

During the first three quarters of 1958, for example, the Soviet Union, as Syria's second biggest customer after Lebanon, bought Syrian goods worth 41,585,000 Syrian pounds (about $10,400,000). During the same period of 1959, the U.S.S.R. ranked thirteenth among Syrian customers and bought only 4,724,000 Syrian pounds (about $1,180,000) worth of goods. Communist China's drop was even more startling—from 23,953,000 pounds (almost $6,000,000) in 1958 to 439,000 pounds ($110,000) in the first three quarters of 1959. Czechoslovakia and Hungary also lowered their imports from Syria.

The speculative reasons for this startling drop in Soviet bloc purchases include Chinese Communist disappointment at failure to find a market in Syria for its own goods, Soviet disgruntlement at the vigor of Syria's internal anti-Communist campaign, and general Communist disillusionment at the failure of the Soviet bloc to penetrate Syria more effectively economically.

Evidences of friction, or mutual suspicion, between Syrians and Soviet officials and technicians in Syria are increasingly frequent. The Syrian region of the U.A.R. passed a law that no foreign purchaser of Syrian cotton could resell this cotton to another country without first obtaining permission from Syria. This provision was aimed at the Soviet practice of buying Syrian and Egyptian cotton and then dumping at least part of it on the world market at low prices. Syrian customs officials, for no visible reason except harassment, are known to have held up for several weeks a personal consignment of liquor to the Soviet consul general in Damascus.

Quite possibly Soviet bloc nations will buy more heavily in the late stages of the current cotton marketing season, thus altering the trade statistics quoted above. Even so a discernible drop in Communist bloc purchases in Syria is evident. So far it could not be called a permanent trend adjusting Syria's trade more favorably with the West.

As in Egypt, so in Syria, the area of technical aid and credit assistance belongs almost exclusively to the Soviet bloc, though the United States has begun to inch its way into this field. Communist credits, totaling $195,000,000 by spring of 1960, had been negotiated beginning in 1957 partly because the Syrian government at that time was pro-Soviet and partly because the credits offered were far cheaper than anything advanced by the West. Of these credits Syria to date has drawn about $70,000,000.

This does not mean that $70,000,000 has been invested in visible projects in Syria. A great deal of this money has been used to pay the per diem expenses of hundreds of Communist technicians in the country. At times this bill has run as high as $20,000 per day. Much of the rest of the $70,000,000 has paid for initial surveys undertaken by Soviet experts prior to the construction stage.

A striking development is the fact that wherever possible the projects resulting from these surveys are being given to non-Soviet firms. One survey completed by the Soviets in December, 1958, was the aerial mapping of Syria at a scale of 1:25,000. The second stage of this project, at a scale of 1:5,000, was given to Italians rather than to Soviets. Observers believe this decision stemmed from the U.A.R.'s reluctance to have the Soviets engaged in such large scale mapping in the U.A.R.'s northern region.

Also envisioned under the Soviet credit agreement of 1957 was the development of the Syrian port of Tartous on the Mediterranean Sea. The U.A.R. chose a Danish firm as consulting engineers and awarded the construction contract to the Yugoslavs—as bad as granting it to a free world firm from the Soviet point of view.

The Soviet loan agreement of 1957 included the drawing up of plans for three thermoelectric plants in Syria—in Damascus, Aleppo, and Homs. The only contract closed at this writing, that for the Damascus plant, was won by the Swiss. This is not to say that no contracts are being awarded to Communist firms. An even longer list could be drawn up of individual construction projects won by the Soviet bloc. But again these firms are East German, Bulgarian, Hungarian and Czechoslovak rather than Soviet.

A leading Syrian industrialist told me privately in Damascus early in 1960 that the U.A.R. government was willing to give Syrian construction firms a 5 per cent advantage in bidding against Communist firms. This means a Syrian bid 5 per cent higher than a corresponding Communist bid still would win the contract.

A flurry of Soviet activity occurred in the spring of 1960 when a Russian delegation surveyed possible new development plans for the Syrian region. How many definite projects may emerge from this survey is not clear, but it seems apparent that most, if not all, of the foreign credits for any new projects will come from the original Soviet aid agreement with Syria. A possible exception is the projected Euphrates River Dam, scheduled to increase Syria's agricultural income by as much as $200,000,000 yearly.

The one inescapable conclusion from all this is that Soviet influence in the Middle East has become permanent through Moscow's military, economic, and technical aid to the United Arab Republic and Iraq, as well as through

Communist trade with these countries. From now on the West, spearheaded by the United States, will face spirited competition in the Middle East, diplomatically and economically. But the battle need not be lost.

In Iraq the government of Premier Abdel Karim Kassem remains infiltrated by Communists in the ministries of national guidance, education, and to some extent planning and agrarian reform. Communists still dominate sections of the labor movement of Iraq, and retain some key posts within the armed forces. But already the Iraqi public has shown its overwhelming preference for Western commercial goods. Meanwhile, the Soviet economic aid program has failed as yet to get off the ground. Finally, the bulk of Iraq's income continues to come from the West through the sale of oil, giving any future anti-Communist government of the country an escape hatch from its commitments to the East.

For President Nasser's United Arab Republic there is no such escape hatch. Only slowly and painfully can Egypt's hard currency earnings be increased to the point that Egypt can afford to buy a measure of Western technological help in place of Communist aid. This growth must come through increased sales of finished cotton textiles to the free world, higher Suez Canal revenues, income from tourism, and other sources, including the United States Point Four program. To the degree that Egypt's industrialization plans can be made to succeed, Cairo's need for expensive foreign machine goods will be reduced.

In Syria the financial problem is somewhat similar, though less crucial because Syria has a wider range of commodities to sell, a much smaller population relative to its cultivable land, and more varied sources of income with which to balance its trade. In both regions of the U.A.R.

the government is disenchanted with the Soviet Union and increasingly considers its own aims incompatible with those of the Communist bloc.

Yemen and Afghanistan are the other significant areas of Soviet penetration of the Middle East. To Yemen the Communist bloc has extended $17,000,000 worth of military credits, all of which have been used, and nearly $42,000,000 worth of economic credits, of which $10,000,-000 have been drawn. These economic credits include a $25,000,000 loan by the Soviet Union and an interest-free loan worth $16,300,000 by Communist China.

Very likely this Communist aid to Yemen spells no real threat to the West, unless the bloc is able to regain the active political support of President Nasser. In that case the tail that is Yemen might wag with the body of the U.A.R., to which it is loosely joined in the so-called United Arab States. For the present, President Nasser's own disquiet at Communist activities encourages similar feeling within Yemen. A notable instance is reported friction between Yemenis and Chinese Communist technicians in the kingdom.

Far larger quantitatively is Communist aid to Afghanistan, which unofficially has been totaled as high as $250,-000,000, including at least $30,000,000 and possibly $75,-000,000 in military aid. (Properly speaking, Afghanistan is part of south Asia but its western face looks toward the Middle East.) As has been noted, the Shah of Iran is deeply concerned lest his kingdom be boxed in between Russian-equipped military forces in Afghanistan on the east and Iraq on the west.

Afghanistan is separated from Iran by extremely difficult mountain and desert terrain. By themselves Afghanistan's armed forces almost certainly could not invade Iran, according to Western experts, even if they were operating in concert with an Iraqi-launched attack on the west. Any potential danger arising from Afghanistan's six new airfields would come from their use by the Soviet Air Force itself. Such use, however, if directed actively against either Pakistan or Iran, would risk world war, since the United States has bilateral defense treaties with both these states.

Perhaps the main benefit to the Soviets from their military aid to Afghanistan has been its use as a wedge to widen the base of their economic support of the country. In the civilian field the Russians made an impact on Afghans by building such visible assets as a giant bakery to service 50,000 persons, gasoline storage tanks, a grain silo, and a flour mill. The Soviets also have embarked on a formidable hydroelectric project on the Kabul River. In the sunshine of this aid Soviet-Afghan trade has blossomed.

Diplomatically the Soviets have sought good will among the Afghans by supporting Afghanistan's demand that the estimated 8,000,000 Pathan tribesmen who live along the Afghan-Pakistani border be allowed to form a state of their own called "Pushtoonistan." Pakistan, which would stand to lose to "Pushtoonistan" a large piece of its territory including the famed Khyber Pass, has refused the demand. This constant irritant between Afghanistan, backed by the Soviet Union, and Pakistan, allied with the United States, is inflamed by Moscow at every opportunity.

In Afghanistan the United States' own large aid program, totaling about $91,000,000 in grants and $51,000,000 in loans, is overshadowed by that of the Soviet Union. It is not that America is in ill repute in Afghanistan; rather that so far Americans have come off second best in impressing the Afghans with their brand of technical and economic assistance. By contrast to the Soviets the Americans have suffered, both from the "invisible" nature of some of the American long-range development work, and because the American-engineered Helmand Valley irrigation and hydroelectric project has failed to meet Afghan expectations. Nonetheless, the Afghan government professes strict neutrality between East and West and by no means has rejected help from the United States.

If the West foresees Soviet domination of Afghanistan by the sheer weight of Moscow's military and economic aid, the Afghans themselves stress their political independence. A leading Iranian official told me that the Iranian government had warned Afghanistan: "When one dines with the devil, he should use a very long spoon." When the Afghans replied that no strings were attached to Russian help, the Iranians returned: "Perhaps later there will be ropes and chains."

In the final analysis, Afghanistan is geographically remote, unsuited as a Soviet access path to richer fields of exploitation. Iraq and the United Arab Republic, by contrast, open directly out on the Persian Gulf and Africa. While the massive Soviet aid program in Afghanistan cannot be discounted, it would appear to pose no crucial threat to Western interests, so long as Iran and Pakistan remain firm allies of the United States.

Here ends the story of real Soviet penetration of the Middle East. It is true that since 1955, Turkey has accepted credits from the Soviet Union worth at least $10,-000,000 to help in the construction of various industrial projects. Iran also has accepted very modest credits from Moscow. Yet these deals failed to lessen the staunch anti-Communist convictions of the governments of the two countries, nor were their alliances with the United States weakened.

With Lebanon, Jordan, Saudi Arabia, the Sudan, and Israel the Communist bloc has at best only minor trade and in some cases no trade, and occasional cultural exchanges with some of these countries. In no case, however, is the basic Westward orientation of these Middle Eastern nations in question.

Violent overthrow of King Hussein of Jordan could benefit the Communists, whose local agents are active among Jordan's huge refugee population. This possible benefit would be greatly reduced if neighboring Iraq were shown to have rejected communism after its republican revolution. Also, President Nasser, as King Hussein's leading Arab enemy, has a vested interest in the stability of Jordan for the present, lest Israel use unrest in Jordan as a reason to advance its eastern frontier to the Jordan River. Since many of King Hussein's detractors at home look toward Cairo for guidance, there appears to be no immediate threat to the Jordanian throne, despite its underlying instability.

# CHAPTER 8

# Challenge to Yankee Traders

Because Soviet penetration of the Middle East is most meaningful in Iraq and the United Arab Republic, it is toward those countries that American efforts must be directed if communism is to be defeated, or at least contained, in the area. Increasingly these American efforts must be economic, if they are to succeed. Not only has Washington been rebuffed by Cairo and Damascus whenever the United States has sought to influence their governments politically, but President Nasser and his colleagues by themselves have recognized the political nature of the Communist threat to the U.A.R.

On the economic side the Soviet Union possesses an enormous advantage, as we have seen, in being able to purchase the Egyptian and Syrian cotton which the U.A.R. must sell. Unlike the United States, the Soviet Government does not protect its domestic cotton growers with import restrictions and subsidies. In 1955 Soviet Premier Khrushchev told a group of United States Congressmen: "We value trade least for economic reasons and most for political purposes."[1] When cotton imports cause a surplus in the U.S.S.R., Moscow merely re-exports its surplus to the world market, often reaping further political gain by undercutting established market prices.

The free world possesses an economic advantage over the Communists in Iraq, where the country's oil flows by pipeline and tanker almost exclusively to the West. In Iraq the Soviets must key their campaign to economic and technical aid, just as the United States is forced to do in the U.A.R.

Year in and year out Egypt depends upon its cotton crop to earn at least 60 per cent of its foreign exchange income. Should this all-important crop fail to move, Egypt would fall desperately behind in its constant struggle to feed its people. A little less than 5 per cent of Egypt's land currently is cultivable. Within this arable area 24,000,000 Egyptians are jammed in one of the densest concentrations on earth.

But this is only part of the story. Egypt's population increases so fast it will double in thirty years. Here is the stark and terrible impetus behind Cairo's almost frantic desire to industrialize itself and to increase arable land through construction of the High Aswan Dam and other reclamation measures. Only thus can President Nasser hope to keep pace with the birth rate of his people. Any early rise in the standard of living of Egypt's people appears almost impossible to achieve.

One qualified Egyptian economist put it this way: Egypt's five-year industrialization plan is scheduled to create 100,000 new industrial jobs. By the end of the five years Egypt's population growth will have provided 900,-

[1] Quoted in "The Sino-Soviet Economic Offensive in Less Developed Countries" (Department of State publication 6632, May, 1958), p. 6.

000 new workers. Even assuming 400,000 of these can be employed on the land—which is unlikely—a gap of 400,000 persons remains. Taking into account all foreseeable Soviet, American, West German, Japanese, and other foreign credits, Egypt herself will have to put up at least $1,000,-000,000 if her industrialization program and High Dam are to be completed as originally scheduled.

This was an Egyptian official speaking in private. In public U.A.R. authorities give a much rosier estimate of the numbers of new jobs to be created in Egypt within the next few years. But even these optimists do not deny that population growth will prevent Egypt's standard of living from rising above its present level.

Adequate birth control, the most logical supplement to industrialization and land reclamation, will be difficult to achieve for many years, given the general opposition of the Moslem clergy and the stolid insistence of the Egyptian fellah that more sons means more hands to do the work. Leading Egyptian officials admit the need for birth control but warn that widespread ignorance, apathy, and opposition must be overcome.

Recently I asked President Nasser his views on the question. He replied that people must be educated to understand why family growth should be limited. He was against government fiat on the problem. This answer was indicative of the gradual and cautious line the U.A.R. government apparently intends to take.

Early in the Syrian-Egyptian merger a joint committee studied the possibility of moving large numbers of Egyptian fellahin from the Nile Valley to Syria's underpopulated but fertile eastern lands. Nothing has come of the plan, presumably because of the human and social disruption involved in forcibly uprooting fellahin from their beloved

Nile banks. Movement of Egyptian peasants southward along the Nile into the Sudan has been frustrated by the opposition of the Sudanese.

Under the circumstances Egyptian planners have no alternative but to devote their efforts to improving conditions at home. Egypt's new class of bureaucrat is made up largely of young Army officers and college graduates. The earnestness with which these people contemplate their tasks is deeply moving. Only in Israel, among Middle Eastern lands, has the author found equal zeal and application to social betterment.

An example of this zeal among Egyptians is seen in the small corps of social workers to whom President Nasser's government has entrusted the gigantic task of reforming the agrarian life of the nation. Since the Agrarian Reform Law was passed September 9, 1952—less than two months after Colonel Nasser's revolutionary junta seized power—565,-000 feddans (a feddan equals 1.038 acres) have been requisitioned from 1,768 landowners and distributed to landless peasants and small farmers in units no larger than five feddans per family.

To service these new landowners, who previously had to rely upon a usurious landlord or middleman, about 275 village cooperative societies have been set up to provide credit for seeds and fertilizer, to market crops, and to provide ancillary services.

Few Egyptian officials would claim that the job has any more than begun, for to transfer ownership of land to the peasants is only the first step in insuring that the peasant adjusts to his new status, and that productivity of the land broken up into small units does not decline. Currently, for example, the Agrarian Reform Organization is struggling to devise a crop rotation schedule to combat the ill effects of land fragmentation resulting from inheritance practices instituted by the Koran and thereby inviolable to Egyptian Moslems. Under this system a piece of land steadily is split into smaller units as heirs inherit a deceased owner's land.

One of the most interesting and possibly the most significant achievements of these agrarian reform workers is the fact that in at least a few Egyptian villages water buffalo now are being insured. Lest this sound facetious, the following facts should be considered:

The average income of an Egyptian peasant is 20 Egyptian pounds or $56 a year. The price of a water buffalo is about 100 Egyptian pounds. By comparison an American worker earning $5,000 annually would need to spend $25,000 to buy an automobile. But to such a worker an automobile would be a luxury. To an Egyptian peasant a water buffalo is an absolute necessity, as motive power for plowing fields and turning water wheels.

Thus in the past, and even today in most of Egypt, many peasants literally placed the welfare of their buffalo ahead of that of their children, for if the buffalo died it could not be replaced, and the entire family would suffer.

In struggling with this aspect of Egypt's farm life, Agrarian Reform Organization officials hit upon an insurance scheme whereby the peasant pays into his village cooperative bank 10 piasters (about 28 cents) a month. In return the peasant receives free medical care for his beast, and should the buffalo die, the farmer receives 75 per cent of the purchase price of a new animal from the cooperative insurance fund.

Strange as it may seem to Westerners accustomed to the purpose of insurance policies, Egyptian peasants did not rush to enter this plan, but had to be persuaded through practical experience to pay out even 10 piasters of their pitiful store of money with no immediate prospects of its return. Today, largely because some peasants actually have received 75 per cent of the purchase price of a new buffalo, the insurance plan is flourishing in a few village cooperative societies. This is truly a major step in lifting the eyes of the Egyptian peasant even slightly above the mud and squalor into which centuries of poverty and feudalistic land practices have ground him.

The story illustrates not only the ingenuity of agrarian reform officials but also the complexities inherent merely in one phase of the Egyptian government's endeavor to make its land resources fit the exploding needs of its rapidly growing population.

Syria has no such problem. Blessed with fertile soil, much of it as yet untouched by a relatively small population, the northern region of the U.A.R. has a potentially sound economy subject only to the vagaries of the weather. In the process of time, as a network of irrigation and water storage works are spread throughout the country, even the recurrent problem of drought can be reduced.

Iraq has the same rich bounty of fertile soil as yet underdeveloped by a population which could double without straining the productive resources of the country. This does not ignore the fact that today Iraq's poverty is abysmal. But, given a reasonable degree of political stability, there is no reason why income from oil cannot gradually harness the Tigris and Euphrates to bring new lands under cultivation.

In neither Syria nor Iraq, in other words, is there any indigenous bar to eventual improvement in living standards. President Nasser might well envy Iraqi leaders their income from oil and their untouched lands. At least the

Egyptian leader can be grateful that his northern region of Syria, except in drought years, is able to sustain itself.

This is the economic background against which American aid and trade operates in Iraq and the United Arab Republic. The United States program in these countries, as well as elsewhere in the Middle East, breaks down into public and private efforts, of which the public effort—that is, direct United States government assistance—is overwhelmingly larger. The private effort embraces commercial trade between American firms and their overseas markets and suppliers, and also technical assistance provided by American companies under contract to foreign governments or private agencies.

United States government programs are ranged beneath the vast umbrella of the Mutual Security Program, for which the President asks a yearly appropriation from Congress. This is the so-called "foreign aid" bill. In recent years President Eisenhower has requested in the order of $4,000,000,000 for mutual security, from which Congress traditionally slices several hundred million dollars before appropriating funds.

Included within the Mutual Security Program (MSP) is all military aid America gives to its overseas allies in the form of military equipment and directly in dollars to help recipient governments meet their defense budgets. The greater part of American aid to Jordan, for example, is "budgetary support," or cash with which Jordan equips and pays for the Jordan Arab Army. This bill alone costs the United States about $40,000,000 yearly.

The second prong of the Mutual Security Program is economic. Here are grouped the Technical Cooperation Program (Point Four); the Development Loan Fund; the President's special contingency fund for emergencies; a

"Special Assistance" fund for projects uncovered by other programs where United States interests are involved; the Investment Guaranty Program, designed to protect private American investors from nonbusiness risks; sales of surplus agricultural products under Public Law 480; United States contributions to international relief agencies; and other classifications.

Each of these programs has its own detailed budget requirements, which, when lumped together, comprise the President's request for economic funds under the Mutual Security Program. Though the array of agencies may seem bewildering, each was developed for a special purpose.

Point Four, for example, is essentially the shipment of American technical know-how overseas, both to train foreign specialists and to implement specific development projects. The Development Loan Fund is a United States government corporation authorized to make "soft" loans; that is, dollar loans repayable in local currencies. Established in June, 1957, the Development Loan Fund supplements the hard currency loans of the World Bank and of the Export-Import Bank, which underdeveloped countries often cannot afford.

Welcomed by many less developed countries are sales of surplus American cereals, principally wheat, under the provisions of Public Law 480, whose operations have been described earlier.

Thus American aid is extended through a wide-ranging complex of lending agencies. The Export-Import Bank is a U.S. government agency dealing in hard currency loans. Its soft currency supplement is the Development Loan Fund, also a government corporation. The World Bank (International Bank for Reconstruction and Development) is a United Nations affiliate, whose total capital is about

55 per cent subscribed by the United States. This bank deals in hard currency loans.

Now in process of formation is the International Development Association (IDA), designed to be a soft currency affiliate of the World Bank. In an effort to widen the international base of the new organization, the United States will subscribe only 32 per cent of IDA's capital, or about $320,000,000. Approximately $440,000,000 in gold or hard currencies is scheduled to be given to IDA by Western Europe, Canada, and Japan. Underdeveloped nations will contribute enough soft currencies to give IDA a total capital subscription of $1,000,000,000.

If the United States has its way, the International Development Association will be confined to members of the World Bank and International Monetary Fund, so that the Soviet bloc will be excluded. Nor will the United Nations itself have a controlling voice over IDA. Congress has proven reluctant to vote foreign aid funds which might be controlled or influenced by the United Nations or the Communist bloc.

Apart from the International Development Association, Washington is urging other industrialized nations of the free world to step up their own bilateral contributions to underdeveloped nations, thus taking some of the burden off the United States. This appeal is aimed not so much at Britain and France, which already contribute substantially overseas, as at West Germany and Japan, whose healthy economies were built up after World War II with United States help.

This request to its allies is inspired by Washington's growing concern over the U.S.'s annual payments deficit, now running close to $4,000,000,000 a year. This means that each year the U.S. spends overseas $4,000,000,000 more than it earns, resulting in a drain on United States' gold reserves. Foreign aid funds contribute heavily to this drain. Eventually it is hoped to decrease American foreign aid spending, but in the meantime Washington would like other nations' contributions to rise at least enough to keep the American outlay from expanding.

On October 19, 1959, the United States took a new departure in its foreign aid program by requiring most future loans by the Development Loan Fund to be spent on American goods. Since the DLF's inception in 1957, nearly half of its loans had been spent by recipient governments for procurement in Europe and Japan, thus contributing to the United States' annual outflow of dollars. By requiring DLF funds to be spent on procurement in the U.S., the outflow of dollar funds through the DLF will be matched by the purchase of American goods. Certain exceptions to the new "buy American" rule were made to avoid hardship, as where a borrowing nation already had invested in foreign equipment which could not be teamed with American manufactures.

In one form or another, and usually in several forms, these American aid programs have been accepted by every Middle Eastern nation with the exception of Syria before its union with Egypt. Today, as the northern region of the United Arab Republic, Syria accepts Public Law 480, Point Four, and Development Loan Fund support. Egypt is a major recipient of such help. The Point Four program is just beginning to edge back into Iraq, as Premier Kassem eases his earlier complete rejection of American support.

The American foreign aid program is presented to Congress as an example of enlightened self-interest. Only when a nation's economy begins to be developed, the administration argues, can that nation become an expanding market for American goods. Such a market requires roads, ports, railways, and telecommunications systems to handle and distribute imports, as well as a citizenry prosperous enough to buy foreign goods. Basically the American aid program is aimed at giving other nations these facilities, as well as bolstering them militarily when they agree to join the free world alliance.

Seen from this standpoint, private American business and the United States government are partners, for business will be benefited as the government's aid programs succeed. In such a spirit of cooperation the U.S. government sends through the world American trade missions staffed by American businessmen and a representative of the United States Department of Commerce. The object of these missions is to promote healthy trade relations between the United States and the nations visited.

At least eighty trade missions have been sent abroad since March, 1955, when President Eisenhower asked Congress for emergency funds permitting the United States to participate in international trade fairs, send trade missions abroad, and otherwise expand American commercial activity overseas. To staff these missions, the Department of Commerce selects businessmen of prominence in various fields and provides them with a round-trip ticket to and from the United States, plus a regular State Department per diem.

The businessman provides his time and services free. He is prohibited from selling the products of his own firm or from setting up any future deals which might benefit his firm. As a "living capitalist" he is expected to explain American business practices to businessmen overseas, make them aware of trade opportunities with the United States, and report back to the American business community on trade conditions in the countries visited.

In February, 1960, a six-man trade mission headed by E. Paul Hawk, director of the Trade Missions Program of the U.S. Department of Commerce, toured the United Arab Republic. The group was keenly aware that political relations between the U.A.R. and the United States were improving. It also was conscious of the imbalance of trade between the two countries because of the United States' inability to purchase large quantities of Egyptian and Syrian cotton and wheat. Given these conditions, the mission's task was to seek ways of bolstering two-way trade to protect and strengthen the friendlier political climate.

To accompany Mr. Hawk the Department of Commerce chose William F. Huck, retired vice president, Bank of America; James Thomas Chirurg, chairman of the board of the James Thomas Chirurg advertising firm of Boston; Thomas J. Carlin, assistant sales manager, American Express Company; Charles J. Kelly, director of Getz Bros. and Co., San Francisco; and Wallace E. Carroll, president of the American Gage and Machine Company, Chicago.

Members of the mission were struck by the preference for American goods which they found among many Syrians and Egyptians. At times this preference was selective. Some Syrian contractors bought American trucks for their chassis and then ripped out the engines in favor of West German or British diesels.

In other cases the preference was pointed up in a way the Syrians may not have intended. Among the bare limestone hills outside of Damascus squats a gray concrete factory, manufacturing detergents. Posters on the factory show a familiar-looking detergent box, orange, yellow, and blue in color, with a housewife surveying snowy lines of laundry.

Name of the detergent is Ride, R-i-d-e. The factory is owned by a Palestinian refugee who, as it happens, also has the Tide agency for Syria. Presumably what he misses on the left hand, he picks up on the right. The Palestinian insists he is infringing no licensing or formula rights, and he may be correct. But certainly he is trading on the name of an American detergent which has become the most popular washday product in Syria.

The liking for American products was reassuring, but by itself it does not solve the problem of two-way trade. For example, Mr. Hawk brought with him a list of sixty-one American firms desiring to increase business with the U.A.R. Only two of those firms expressed an interest in importing U.A.R. products into the States. The other fifty-nine wanted to sell their output in the U.A.R.

Despite this trend the touring Americans concluded there were several feasible ways in which the U.A.R. could earn more dollars and so reduce somewhat its trade gap with the United States. One possibility was the licensing of U.A.R. firms to produce American "name" products for sale within the Arab market. Arrow shirts, for instance, cannot enter Egypt because of Egypt's need to save dollars. But a steady demand for Arrow shirts is believed to exist within Egypt.

Why not, then, license an Egyptian company to manufacture Arrow shirts, using Egyptian cotton and adhering to American standards of manufacture, with the Arrow Company receiving a percentage of the sales? Numbers of such opportunities for licensing rights exist in Egypt and Syria, trade mission members believed, with the arrangements to be individually made by the Arab and American firms in question.

(To some degree Syrian businessmen benefit from currency control regulations which exclude the import of certain foreign products into Egypt. Importation of some of these goods is permissible in Syria. The goods then are resold to Egypt in legal transactions between two regions of the same country.)

Another possibility suggested was that U.A.R. firms manufacture parts which then would be shipped to the United States for assembly with American-made parts into a whole piece of machinery or other product, with the Arab-made part "invisible." The attraction of this system, which already exists between the United States and some other countries, would be the low cost of labor in Egypt and Syria. Again, an American patent owner with a wholly internal market might lease manufacturing rights to an Arab firm for sale in the foreign market.

Already the U.A.R. is being encouraged by the United States to convert more of its raw cotton into finished textile products. Shirts and blouses of high grade Egyptian long staple cotton find a ready market in the United States, while a volume market is believed to exist for garments made of lower grade cotton whose price tags would reflect lower labor costs in Egypt. To give substance to this encouragement, American buyers bought $20,000,000 worth of finished cotton textiles from Egypt in 1959.

Tourism could be a prime dollar earner for both regions of the U.A.R., though trade mission members stressed the U.A.R. first must reduce the frustrating red tape and suspicion which often greet Western visitors to Syria and Egypt. The trade group realized that tension between Israel and the U.A.R. and among Arab states themselves militated against lowered surveillance of visitors. Even so there were certain steps considered possible at the moment.

A unified tourist bureau might be set up for both regions of the country. This bureau then could "sell" the U.A.R. as a whole and the tourist attractions of Lebanon and Jordan as well. But ill feeling between Jordan and the U.A.R. might jeopardize this venture, though both sides would benefit from mutual advertising.

The trade mission heard frequent complaints that the U.A.R. received a bad press in the United States. It was suggested that the Arabs hire a professional public relations firm to offer free factual articles to American publications, describing individual development or industrial projects underway or completed in the U.A.R. Or, to save dollars, such articles could be written by American-trained Egyptian and Syrian writers. Trade and business papers in the U.S. might welcome such contributions, it was felt.

U.A.R. tourist authorities, with a wealth of historical attractions in their country, should offer "package tours" with special off-season rates to teacher and student groups in the United States as well as Europe. In this respect, it was pointed out, a West German mark or British pound sterling or other hard currency was as valuable to earn as a dollar, since all these currencies were freely convertible. Thus the U.A.R. did not need to achieve a dollar-for-dollar sale to the United States in order to reduce its trade gap.

Since visas are a nuisance to the traveler, their irritant quotient should be reduced. A folder handed out with the visa would seek the visitor's good will by pointing out why the U.A.R. still considered visas necessary, and explaining that apparently irksome restrictions were not aimed at the tourist. Another folder, perhaps signed in President Nasser's name, would bid the traveler a cordial farewell when he left the U.A.R. Attached to the folder might be a small packet of the U.A.R.'s handsome postage stamps.

Over and over again members of the trade mission were met by the plea from Arab businessmen for better credit terms on which to buy American machinery. Despite a genuine preference for American and other Western machinery, U.A.R. contractors often were forced to buy Communist-bloc equipment because of the lower prices and easier credit offered. Particularly hard hit by this, the trade group was told, were Syrian and Egyptian contractors eager to bid on their country's development projects but hampered by the high cost of American machinery they would like to use. Members of the trade mission found many Arabs willing to pay higher prices for American goods but demanding the kind of easy credit which would permit them to pay those higher prices.

With this plea American businessmen are in complete agreement. But they contend they cannot offer easier credit until the United States government backs them up with a wider investment guaranty program. As it now stands, American firms not only are outbid by the Communists, but often by British and West German salesmen, whose governments insure them substantially against loss in the foreign market.

The United States already has an Investment Guaranty Program, whose funds form part of the omnibus foreign aid bill and are administered through the International Cooperation Administration (Point Four). This program is designed to protect the American businessman from three types of risks in a foreign country—expropriation or confiscation of property, war, and nonconvertibility of currency.

Should a foreign government seize an American company's property and fail to pay proper compensation, the United States government would pay the insured American firm and negotiate on a government-to-government level for restitution. This kind of government protection can be bought by an American firm at one-half per cent per clause, or one and one-half per cent for triple coverage. At present Washington has bilateral investment guaranty agreements of this type with forty-two nations.

The U.S. government-owned Export-Import Bank and Development Loan Fund, as well as the World Bank, are other credit agencies to which foreign buyers and American firms may apply. But these banking institutions cannot offer the "easy" credit which U.A.R. contractors seek and which would enable American firms to compete more successfully on the Arab market.

A leading recommendation of trade missions such as that led by Mr. Hawk is that the United States government broaden its investment guaranty program by insuring American firms against a wider variety of foreign market risks than now is the case.

President Eisenhower showed awareness of this need when he told Congress in March, 1959:

In order to encourage increased private investment in these areas (Asia and Africa), our Government has already undertaken a system of guarantees against loss from non-convertibility of foreign currency receipts and from expropriation, confiscation, and war. To further stimulate such investment, I now request that legislation be enacted to allow similar guarantees against risks of revolution, insurrection, and related civil strife. I propose also that the Congress double the availability of such guarantees.[2]

The above points relate primarily to what the United States government and Arab governments can do to foster a healthier balance of trade between the two sides. But in the over-all effort to make the American economic contribution to the Middle East more meaningful, a share of the responsibility falls on private American firms. Some supposedly hard-headed Yankee traders appear to have a good deal to learn if they are to increase their own overseas earnings, as well as contribute to the defeat of communism in the area. This is pointed up by current experience in Iraq.

General Kassem's regime still virtually excludes United States government aid programs from Iraq. Even should this situation change, seasoned American observers in Baghdad believe it might be a mistake for Washington to rush in with new official aid. As matters now stand, the Soviets are becoming increasingly identified with economic failure in Iraq. There is no disposition in the American Embassy in Baghdad to pull Soviet chestnuts out of the fire by pumping in American aid, at least before the Iraqi people have had a good chance to weigh their experience with the Communists.

Besides, Iraq's development program has fallen so completely apart that even United States help could not provide much immediate visible improvement. Thus American technicians on the scene might provide hard-pressed Iraqi officials with another foreign scapegoat to hide their own shortcomings.

[2] From the President's Message to Congress dated March 13, 1959, as quoted in "The Mutual Security Program: Fiscal Year 1960," an official publication of the Department of State, p. xix.

This leaves the current field largely to private American firms, if United States influence is to weigh more effectively in Iraq than it does today. Iraqi importers, now freed by their government to purchase goods where they will, are showing active interest in what Americans have to offer. At the same time Iraqis are showing interest in what other Western countries have to sell. It is this kind of competition that will force American companies to improve their performance if their share of the Iraqi market is to be enlarged, or even maintained.

Much depends on the quality of agent the American company hires to represent it in Iraq. In the pre-Kassem era American products were in such demand that many U.S. manufacturers had little "selling" to do. All they needed was an agent capable of accepting and filling orders. Such agents often took little or no responsibility for providing service and spare parts for their customers, once the goods had been delivered. Today this kind of agent is worse than useless to an American firm, and may be the cause of prospective buyers taking their trade elsewhere.

In the fall of 1959, the Iraqi government circularized the business community, asking for bids on an industrial plant it was planning to build. The government asked for complete specifications on equipment, including internal floor plans where the equipment was to be installed. Until these floor plans were received, the government would not design its buildings.

The Iraqi in charge of the project, trained in the United States himself, talked with the local agent of an American firm manufacturing some of the world's finest equipment of the type needed. Pointing out the importance of the potential order, the man in charge of the project suggested a cable to the home office. The agent replied that a cable might cost sixty dinars—$168—and that he would airmail a letter. The agent was not a technician and appeared unaware of the implications of the project.

Seven months later the American corporation had not sent in specifications. British and West German competitors, meanwhile, had submitted handsome brochures complete down to the last details. When the Iraqi government stressed that Iraqi operators would need to be trained in the use of whatever equipment was chosen, the American company suggested trainees be sent to France or Italy. Iraq has no diplomatic relations with France, and Italian technicians probably could not instruct in English.

As this book goes to press, bids have not been closed on the project and it is possible the American specifications will arrive. But the point remains that, through poor choice of dealer and lack of information about current Iraqi business, the American corporation was outclassed by its European competitors, two of whom maintained their own European representatives in Baghdad. The American firm's Baghdad agent was at fault for not keeping his employers abreast of what the post-revolution Iraqi market demanded, and for lacking vision to see that a relatively small investment on his part, coupled with active promotion, might produce a handsome commission for him.

Two American car manufacturers who maintain spirited competition at home also compete in Iraq. The company which makes "X" car has as its dealer an alert Jewish-Moslem agency in Baghdad which has captured 40 per cent of the Iraqi foreign car market. This agency learned that Premier Kassem's regime, after freezing imports of foreign cars, was about to issue new import licences. Immediately the dealer arranged with "X" company in the United States to produce 115 sedans to his specifications, to be delivered at such and such a date to dockside on the Atlantic coast.

Three days after the cars arrived at the eastern seaboard, import permits were issued in Baghdad. The dealer cabled to the United States and the cars were on their way, months before competitor "Y" would have cars in Iraq.

"Y" company, by comparison, lost its Jewish agent in Baghdad in 1948 when he was expelled from Iraq. Since that time "Y" has changed dealers frequently, but until 1955 had sent out no senior official from the States to assess the situation for himself. Finally "Y" company obtained an Iraqi agent every bit as aggressive and alert as the agent representing "X." Since that time "Y" has put heavy pressure on its new agent to catch up with the Jewish-Moslem representative of "X."

"Y's" new agent won an order for a number of trucks from the Iraqi Ministry of Defence. On international tenders the Iraqi Ministry of Defence pays 75 per cent of the total at the time the contract is signed and the remaining 25 per cent when the equipment is delivered. The Baghdad dealer took his order to "Y's" regional office in Beirut. There the order was refused on the grounds it had not been paid in full. Helpless to change Ministry of Defence regulations, "Y's" agent finally paid the 25 per cent himself rather than lose the order.

Upset by this among other things, the dealer almost threw over "Y" in favor of Mercedes Benz. Through a cable to the Department of Commerce the American Embassy informed "Y" it was in danger of losing an excellent dealer and probably its entire Iraqi market. The situation was patched up, but only after U.S. government intervention with an American company noted for its aggressive sales know-how at home.

By contrast there are other companies operating efficiently in Iraq because they are willing to spend the money
needed to know the situation at first hand. Their American
representatives come to Baghdad prepared to promote their
product as thoroughly as they would in an American
market. Generally these firms have been dealing in the
foreign market for many years, and in some cases regard
the overseas field as their major sales outlet.

Only in the U.A.R. and Iraq, among Middle Eastern
states, does the United States have a real problem in com-
peting with the Communists economically. In the U.A.R.
America's emphasis of necessity is on government-to-government programs, since the Egyptian and Syrian markets
are hampered in private dealings by lack of foreign exchange.

In Iraq it is the other way around. There are good
reasons for the United States government to stay in the
background and let American businessmen do the front
running. But the peculiar requirements of the Iraqi market
must be learned by American companies, if they are to
win their fair share of the market.

# CHAPTER 9

# For Today and Tomorrow

Ein Merissi in Beirut is a street of color. Largely untouched by the building craze running rampant elsewhere in the city, Ein Merissi's old stone walls and courtyards run down to the sea, enclosing houses whose concrete walls have weathered gently to the color of rust. There is no grass, only hard-packed earth within the courtyards, but here and there the outlook is softened by the foliage of an olive or orange tree planted within a walled yard.

From the land side Ein Merissi is at its most attractive, for, truth to tell, at the water's edge the street looks somewhat down at heel. Refuse is often thrown from the balconies of the taller houses, and what the sea fails to carry away bobs among the moss-covered rocks along the shore.

Midway along Ein Merissi an inlet of the sea pierces through to the street, and here Arab fishermen bring in their boats just after dawn, carrying the fish they have caught offshore during the night. Worn stone steps wind up from the inlet to a platform of gleaming white tile set in an old wall running along the street. On this tile the fishermen spread their catch, washed down with buckets of sea water to keep it fresh. The fish sells quickly to the housewives and fishmongers of the district, and by mid-morning the fishermen have scrubbed down the tiles and are back along the shore, drying and mending their nets in the sun before quitting for the day.

These are not the only fishermen of Ein Merissi. One morning I spied half a mile offshore a typical double-ended fishing craft, riding low in the water and being rowed slowly toward shore by two men, each straining at an oar. Over the gunwale hung an odd white shape which I could not make out.

As the boat crept toward another inlet on Ein Merissi, a tall young Arab in green sweater and sea boots gave a piercing whistle and disappeared over the sea wall toward a concrete landing below. At his whistle other Arabs left their coffee in tiny shops and hurried down to the inlet. By the time the boat sidled up to the landing, its gunwale low in the water, a cluster of men milled about on the dock. The cause of their excitement was plain.

Lashed lifeless along the gunwale lay a huge shark, almost as long as the boat. The white shape I had seen was the triangular underside of its head projecting above the gunwale. Laughing and shouting, nine men seized the ropes and heaved the great fish onto the landing. The skin of the shark rasped like sandpaper on the rough concrete. One of the men prodded the shark with his foot and a shudder ran through the long shape, whether from dead muscular reaction or a last gasp of life, I could not tell. Most startling of all were the staring lidless eyes—brilliantly green, the emerald green of deep water in a cavern, shot through by a shaft of light.

Slowly, a foot at a time, leaving a trail of dark red blood behind it, the shark was hauled up a flight of narrow steps to the street, where a truck waited to cart it away to be sold as food. That afternoon on Ein Merissi I saw the giant tail section, like a great scimitar curved up against the wall, resting on a box to be sold. The flesh inside looked white as cream.

As if this were not enough for one street, Ein Merissi is colorful in still another way at certain times of the year. February 22 is the anniversary date of the union between Syria and Egypt, and every year since the merger President Nasser has gone up to Syria to lead the celebrations. This causes a great stir among Lebanon's Moslems, and each February hundreds of them trek over the mountains to visit the President when he is in Damascus.

Ein Merissi is a Moslem street and on the anniversary of the U.A.R. merger the street breaks out in gay bunting, strung from side to side of the road. Shops blossom with pictures of President Nasser and from wires overhead the U.A.R. President smiles benignly down, in full color, as if this were Cairo and not Beirut. Some residents of Ein Merissi thoughtfully put up pictures of Lebanon's President Chehab as well, but mostly along the street President Nasser looks down alone.

This kind of thing is highly unsettling to Lebanese authorities, since tension between Moslem and Christian Lebanese, always latent, rose dangerously to the surface during the Lebanese civil war of 1958. Ein Merissi is not the only street which celebrates the Syrian-Egyptian merger. So do other Moslem sections of Beirut, as well as such Moslem Lebanese towns as Tripoli in the north and Tyre and Sidon in the south. For the Lebanese government to send in troops to haul down the bunting and the pictures might touch off a new round of trouble, yet to permit images of President Nasser to remain plastered on the walls of Moslem shops and homes is a tacit admission that the U.A.R. leader may be more popular with many Lebanese than their own President Chehab.

Quite apart from the dilemma of the Lebanese government, the pro-Nasser demonstrations in Ein Merissi and elsewhere are an indication of Nasser's popular following outside his own country. Here a distinction between Arab leaders and their peoples must be made. President Nasser is anything but popular with many Arab leaders, including, of course, the disgruntled ex-President of Lebanon, Camille Chamoun, and his followers.

Already described have been the efforts of Crown Prince Feisal to undercut President Nasser's popularity among Saudi Arabs. By a relatively austere fiscal program, including putting the royal princes on strict allowances, the Crown Prince has restored a sense of responsibility to the Saudi Government, and possibly to the royal house. But there is no reason to believe that Mr. Nasser, as the outstanding leader of Arab nationalism, has lost his attraction for many Saudi Arab citizens.

Enmity between Nasser and King Hussein is scarcely concealed, despite the U.A.R. leader's cessation of overt efforts to unseat Hussein in favor of a pro-Nasser republic in Jordan. Those efforts, which reached a peak during 1957, failed largely because of the fierce and stubborn loyalty to King Hussein of the Bedouin core of the Jordan Arab Army.

Partly because of this loyalty, and partly because a sadder and wiser Nasser has no desire to shoulder the staggering economic burdens of Jordan, King Hussein's throne appears at least temporarily secure. There is every reason to suppose, however, that many Jordanian hearts still burn warmly for President Nasser, particularly among King Hussein's former Palestinian subjects.

As for personal relations between Hussein and Nasser, it seems scarcely conceivable they can lose their present hostility, despite the fact their two countries resumed diplomatic relations in August, 1959. Hussein cannot forgive Nasser's attempts to force him from his throne, and possibly to kill him. Nasser refuses to regard Hussein as anything more than the upstart grandson of a king for whom the British created a throne and country. To President Nasser, the kingdom of Jordan remains an avenue for Western penetration and manipulation in the Middle East, if only because Jordan could not survive without extensive foreign subsidy.

It seems a tragedy these two attractive, intelligent Arab leaders cannot work together in harness. During 1959 I was received by both men—by King Hussein in his white palace on a hill above Amman, and by Mr. Nasser in his suburban Cairo home. With both of them I spoke English. No written questions were submitted in advance. Each replied in excellent English, thoughtfully, aware of the nuances of my questions, never for a moment losing his poise and dignity.

King Hussein is short, handsome, with a deep and pleasant voice. President Nasser is a tall man, somewhat heavier than when he seized power in 1952, but nonetheless forceful and vigorous, with touches of gray at his temples. Both men are impressive, possessed of obvious ability. How much better for their peoples if their talents were devoted to working jointly for the Arab cause, rather than against each other!

As recently as June, 1960, the two men indulged in a renewed public exchange of vicious slander. In a speech at Alexandria on June 24, President Nasser declared there were "still a few traitors in the Arab world who inherited their kingdoms from their fathers and grandfathers." The first duty of the Arabs, the U.A.R. leader said, was "to get rid of these imperialist agents."[1] Despite the virulence of this attack, observers believed it signaled no change from Nasser's policy of maintaining, or enduring, the *status quo* in Jordan, since any change might thrust unwelcome responsibilities on Cairo.

King Hussein replied June 26 by accusing President Nasser of having jumped "to power by plots, cunning, deception, and betrayal of friends and ethics."[2] Caustically the King advised the U.A.R. leader to look back to history "so that he might see an example of the definitive end of every opportunist dictator." Throughout history, Hussein said, "the world has seen the emergence of dictatorships by men mostly of a higher calibre, heavier weight, higher standing, and more straightforward ethics than the President [Nasser], but they all collapsed."[3]

Over the years Mr. Nasser has deeply alienated another able pro-Western Arab leader, President Bourguiba of Tunisia. In March, 1958, Tunis accused Cairo of plotting to assassinate the Tunisian President and overthrow his government. In December of the same year Tunisia's High Court passed death sentences on nine men—five were later commuted to life imprisonment by President Bourguiba— for complicity in this alleged plot. Particularly rankling to Mr. Bourguiba was President Nasser's granting of asylum

[1] *New York Herald Tribune*, June 24, 1960.
[2] Arab News Agency in a dispatch from Amman, June 26, 1960.
[3] *Ibid.*, June 26, 1960.

to Bourguiba's Tunisian enemy, Salah Ben Youssef, author of the alleged plot against the Tunisian President.

In a subsequent conciliatory move the United Arab Republic offered to expunge from Arab League minutes anti-Bourguiba statements made by U.A.R. delegates. Even this failed to soothe Mr. Bourguiba, and the Tunisian leader has made no move toward reconciliation with President Nasser.

Sudan, Egypt's neighbor to the south, long has appeared to be a glittering prize to President Nasser for the immediate and compelling reason that every drop of Egypt's precious Nile water flows through the Sudan, and also because control of the Sudan by Cairo would extend Mr. Nasser's direct influence to the borders of Ethiopia, Kenya, Uganda, the Congo Republic, and French Equatorial Africa.

Rebuffed in his probing moves by the Sudan's pro-Western Premier Abdullah Khalil, Nasser appeared in the fall of 1958 to have made an end run around Mr. Khalil and enlisted the friendship of leading Sudanese politicians. But at this moment a Sudanese Army officer named Lt. Gen. Ibrahim Abboud seized power in a bloodless coup and proceeded to maintain a courteous but cool distance between himself and Mr. Nasser. Though General Abboud, now Sudanese Premier, has come to an amicable Nile Waters agreement with the U.A.R., a prime motive of General Abboud's rule appears to be to prevent the huge but backward Sudan from being swallowed or even dominated by Egypt.

Mr. Nasser has sought to overthrow the President of Tunisia and the King of Jordan—and has failed. In Iraq, Egypt's traditional rival for top Arab leadership, Mr. Nasser still is engaged in a pitched battle for supremacy with

Premier Abdel Karim Kassem. The energy of Nasser's agents and the strength of his popular following throughout the Arab world did contribute to changes of governments in the Sudan, Saudi Arabia, and Lebanon, while Syria, of course, became the northern region of Mr. Nasser's own country.

In Saudi Arabia's Crown Prince Feisal, Lebanon's President Chehab, and General Abboud of the Sudan, President Nasser has found men personally somewhat more cordial to him than the leaders these men replaced. Though this might appear to be an asset for Mr. Nasser, in practice it probably is not, at least so far as his possible desires for expansion are concerned. None of the new leaders mentioned—Feisal, Chehab, or Abboud—has shown the slightest inclination to subordinate his country's independence to President Nasser's control. And all three of the new leaders possess wider local bases of popular support than did the men they replaced, thus offering Mr. Nasser lessened scope for any subversive activities he might attempt.

In addition, President Nasser by no means has won the battle for Syria. This does not mean the U.A.R.'s northern province is threatening to break away from Egypt, despite the evident lack of affection between Syrians and Egyptians generally. Occasional reports filtering out of Syria of clashes between Syrian and Egyptian officers, or of mutiny among isolated Syrian military units—reports containing an element of truth—should not be interpreted as heralding a mass uprising against Cairo's rule.

President Nasser's support among the great peasant base of the Syrian population, and among certain urban elements, remains widespread and enthusiastic. Those Syrians who opposed, and who still regret, the merger of Egypt and Syria—land owners, bankers, industrialists, merchants —have little popular support of their own. They also cast a fearful eye eastward toward the economic chaos and political terror of Iraq, as the likely alternative for Syria should Mr. Nasser's grip weaken.

By the battle for Syria I mean Cairo's ability gradually to turn the present union into a partnership of equal members, each working out its separate economic destiny according to its special conditions—without having made it appear that the merger has failed. The brave talk of unifying the two economies which accompanied the early days of the U.A.R. now has been muted. Currency unification has been shelved. The accumulated experience of Syrian merchants and farmers is being listened to by Cairo, and more and more the Syrian economy is being allowed to follow its natural bent, rather than be squeezed into whatever mold Egyptian economists think might best complement Egypt's own endeavors.

If this smacks of federation rather than tight union, such may not be inconsistent with long-range Egyptian thinking. Through such a solution President Nasser's political hegemony over Syria would remain secure, while total responsibility for managing the Syrian economy would not fall on inexperienced Egyptian shoulders. A possible danger here is that Mr. Nasser might feel he needed the acquisition of one other country to "cover" the easing of Syria back toward a federative status.

In such an event—and I do not mean to imply it is likely —Libya looms as a logical candidate. This geographically huge nation has a population only slightly in excess of 1,000,000 persons. Its economy is backward, and many Libyans feel little sense of identity with their government. Egyptian schoolteachers in Libyan schools afford a channel for enhancing President Nasser's already considerable popular following among Libya's depressed people. Libya is Egypt's western neighbor, offering both relative ease of penetration and excuse for federation. Finally, Libya possesses immense deposits of oil.

To sum up, President Nasser's popularity among other Arab leaders ranges from dubious to nonexistent, while his hold on popular Arab thought remains substantial. This popular approval should not be doubted merely because some Arab leaders inveigh against Mr. Nasser and their peoples raise no objection. Little has occurred to lower Nasser permanently in the estimation of the Moslems of Lebanon, the Palestinians of Jordan, the Army officers and soldiers of Saudi Arabia, the emerging middle class in all Arab lands, eager for a supranational Arab hero.

Even in Iraq, where Kassem's enmity causes Mr. Nasser's picture to appear only when attached to the body of a donkey, many Arab nationalists continue to look toward the U.A.R. President for leadership. "Where else can we look?" one Iraqi Baath Party leader asked me in Baghdad, while sadly acknowledging that Nasser was minimizing Baath influence in Syria. "There is no other leader on the horizon." A senior American diplomat in Baghdad told me he thought it would take no more than one week for Iraqi crowds to be shouting in the streets for President Nasser, if Iraqi propaganda at the top should change.

American observers in the Middle East, both diplomatic and private, are convinced that United States interests in the area cannot be served without at least modest cooperation with the man who is the acknowledged leader of Arab nationalism. This is mere recognition that President Nasser is the single most powerful man in the Arab world, and that it would appear impossible to work harmoniously with the Arabs without the cooperation of Mr. Nasser.

American policy in the Middle East is not all of a piece, but is made up of several separate strands, some of which come perilously close to incompatibility with others. One strand is substantial United States support of King Hussein. Another is cooperation with the royal house of Saudi Arabia. Neither monarchy is liked by President Nasser, or by Israel. But American support of the kings is accepted, because neither Cairo nor Tel Aviv wishes to risk the results of trying to change the *status quo* in Jordan or Saudi Arabia.

Israel and the U.A.R. do not complain about American relations with the remaining Arab states, nor about Washington's formal alliances with Turkey and Iran. Indeed, Turkey and Iran are friendly with Israel, and being non-Arab countries, they do not threaten President Nasser's concept of "positive neutrality" for the Arabs.

What makes America's Middle Eastern policy hazardous is the attempt to be friendly both with Israel and the United Arab Republic. Such dual friendship can be made at least tolerable so long as neither side moves militarily against the other, and so long as Zionist influence in the United States does not produce Congressional action damaging to the United Arab Republic.

There is no question of canceling America's established friendship with Israel. But there should be equally little question about cutting Washington's still fragile ties with Cairo, if United States interests are to be served. Controversy over Washington's Palestine policy lies in the past. Disagreement over the United States government's attempt to cooperate with President Nasser is fresh, and the policy bears examination.

Principal objections to Mr. Nasser are that he is anti-Western and an enemy of Israel. To many Americans these charges raise the serious question of whether Israel, Britain, King Hussein, and other allies of the United States will be injured by American cooperation with President Nasser. In other words, must the United States sacrifice the interests of other nations to get along with Cairo?

In a situation as complex as that involving Israel, in which emotions on both sides have been stirred to their deepest levels, it would be absurd to say one "knows" that cooperation with President Nasser will not produce additional danger to Israel. One cannot be sure. But if the problem is to be seen in proper perspective, it should be regarded strictly from the standpoint of the United States' national interests. Americans may rest assured that Israel and Britain, as well as other nations deeply interested in the Nasser question, are regarding the problem in the light of their own national interests.

The question of American relations with President Nasser acquired particular pertinence when the Cairo leader began his anti-Communist campaign in December of 1958. On the one hand Mr. Nasser's enemies—primarily, though not exclusively, King Hussein of Jordan within the Arab world, and Israel without—have continued to assert that the leopard has not changed his spots and that President Nasser's anticommunism is a temporary expedient.

On the other hand many Middle Eastern observers of equal authority and experience assert that Mr. Nasser's present rift with the Communists gives the West an unparalleled opportunity to put itself back in line with the main stream of Arab thought, thereby increasing the chances that communism will be defeated in the Middle East.

President Nasser remains, and presumably will remain, fundamentally opposed to Israel. Naturally this colors the views of Israelis, whose very existence is at stake in the hostile Arab world. But it would not seem true that Mr. Nasser's hostility to Israel must preclude cooperative agreements between him and the United States. He is no more anti-Israel than is King Hussein of Jordan, with whom the United States maintains close and friendly relations. Nor is President Nasser any more outspokenly opposed to Israel than are King Saud and Crown Prince Feisal of Saudi Arabia. Both Saudi Arabia and Jordan receive American aid, including military equipment, despite their hostility to Israel.

Admitting this, many Israelis contend that Mr. Nasser is the most powerful of their foes, and that aid to him is more threatening to Israel than is similar aid to Saudi Arabia and Jordan. Thus Israelis are convinced that an Arab world dominated by President Nasser would reduce Israel's chances of achieving a modus vivendi with its neighbors in the Middle East. Again, no one can say for certain this would not be so.

The blunt fact must be faced that Israel, and only Israel, has it within her power to dissipate Arab hostility by implementing her share of United Nations resolutions on Palestine, particularly the General Assembly resolution of December 11, 1948, which "resolves that the refugees wishing to return to their homes and live in peace with their neighbors should be permitted to do so at the earliest practicable date," and that compensation for their lost property should be paid to those who did not choose to return.

Israel claims that the operative phrase here is "live at peace with their neighbors," and that the flood of refugees who might return would be so hostile toward the Jews as to threaten the security of the state. This might be so, though the prospect of cash compensation—which the United States already has indicated it would make available—might dissuade substantial numbers of Palestine Arabs from returning "home."

In any case, the Israeli objection does not dissolve the fact that the resolution is as binding on Israel as the Security Council resolution of September, 1951, enjoining freedom of passage through the Suez Canal, is binding on President Nasser. Juridically, Israel and the United Arab Republic are equally at fault in their obligations toward UN resolutions.

In an interview with another American correspondent and myself on October 7, 1959, Mr. Nasser declared his willingness to allow Israeli shipping through the Suez Canal, provided Israel obeyed other UN resolutions detailing the rights of the Arabs of Palestine. Specifically Mr. Nasser said he would accept a United Nations board to implement all resolutions passed by that body pertaining to the Palestine problem. When the interview was published, Israel dismissed the proposal largely as a Cairo propaganda gambit. For special reasons, I do not believe it was.

Some time before the interview took place, I had been informed that President Nasser desired to make a positive statement on the Arab-Israeli dispute, a statement that would improve his moral posture with the American public in particular. I was further informed that the President might be willing to make such a statement through an interview with me. It was suggested I go from my Beirut headquarters to Cairo and there contact Mohammed Heykal, editor of *Al-Ahram* and Nasser's principal press adviser.

I did so, and Mr. Heykal and I discussed the project in the following general terms. The "normalization" process between Cairo and Washington had been proceeding at that time about eighteen months. Necessarily, however, it had been a quiet process, and the image of Nasser in the American public eye had not been enhanced. If that image were to be improved, it might be done through a statement declaring:

1. That Nasser desired to obey the United Nations, conscience of the world.

2. That Mr. Nasser could not do so on the Suez Canal issue, unless Israel obeyed equally pertinent resolutions.

3. That Nasser, therefore, was ready to obey all resolutions if Israel would do the same.

Mr. Nasser was anxious not to slight American correspondents resident in Cairo, Mr. Heykal informed me, and there was a possibility another reporter would receive the interview with me. Subsequently Mr. Heykal called me to say the interview had been set up, and that it would not be inappropriate to advance questions relating to our earlier discussion. Wilton Wynn of the Associated Press would share the interview with me.

The interview was held in the study of Mr. Nasser's Cairo home on the evening of October 7, 1959, and was published the next day. It is quite possible, as some observers since have held, that President Nasser advanced his proposal in the belief Israel would reject it and that no responsibility for doing anything would devolve upon Cairo.

It is also possible that here was an opportunity to break the dangerous stalemate between Arabs and Israelis. Had Israel accepted the offer of a UN board to implement all Palestine resolutions, President Nasser would have had no alternative but to comply. I personally believe negotiations under the aegis of a UN board might have modified some of the most awkward and outdated features of the resolutions, and that a start might have been made toward abolishing the armistice agreements in favor of peace treaties.

But Israeli spokesmen did reject the proposal, and nothing more could be done. As a source close to Mr. Nasser later said: "Nasser cannot nibble at his own bait. Someone else must take the next step." So far that next step remains untaken.

The second objection frequently heard to American cooperation with President Nasser is that he remains anti-Western. He is certainly anti-Western in his opposition to the slightest degree of Western control over Arab policy. President Nasser has worked to oust the British from his own country and from Jordan, and will continue to work against the British position along the Arabian littoral. This fact tends to dominate the British estimate of Nasser, since, quite apart from the element of national pride, Britain depends vitally upon the oil of the Persian Gulf sheikdoms.

But there is ample evidence, documented in earlier chapters, that Mr. Nasser welcomes economic and technical aid from the United States, unconnected with any political conditions, to help him in meeting Egypt's staggering economic problems. Such aid is important within Egypt itself, for the specific good it does to desperately poor people.

Throughout the Arab world this help also fosters the impression that President Nasser and the United States, each without sacrificing principle, have found it possible to get along together. Such an impression helps to mitigate

the suspicion that the United States opposes Arab nationalism and it bolsters Nasser's prestige among many anti-
Communist Arabs in other lands.

Within some quarters in the State Department there
still is a tendency to say: "Has Nasser learned his lesson?
If so, perhaps we can deal with him." This would seem to
mean: Is Nasser now willing to abandon his "positive
neutrality," and his attacks on pro-Western Arab leaders?
(The author is acquainted with many American diplomats
in the Middle East, and very few of them share this
tendency.)

The answer to the question posed is no. To President
Nasser "positive neutrality," or nonalignment of the
U.A.R., is the Arabs' only escape from domination by one
big power bloc or the other. This is a cardinal principle
of his philosophy and it is futile to expect him to abandon
it.

From the standpoint of the United States, it almost certainly would be harmful if Mr. Nasser did desert this
position and come over to "our side." Such a change would
give his enemies, in this context principally the Communists, grounds for charging his desertion from the ranks of
Arab nationalists. As it is now, American help to "neutralist" Mr. Nasser accomplishes the end of friendly relations between Cairo and Washington, without exposing
either side to undue attack.

Mr. Nasser cannot be expected to cease his opposition
to the pro-Western stance of the remaining kings of the
Arab Middle East, since to Mr. Nasser the pro-Western
kings provide an avenue through which the West can continue to infiltrate its control over Arab affairs. Beyond
this, President Nasser is fundamentally suspicious of royalty, partly because of his humble birth in an Egyptian

village, and partly because of Egypt's experience with its own corrupt dynasty.

Also, however painful this may seem to many Americans, King Hussein and King Saud represent political anachronisms hanging on against the winds of change. It is they, not President Nasser, who are out of step with the procession of Arab thought. Washington's alliance with the kings may in the long run be a thornier problem for American foreign policy than the United States' developing cooperation with Nasser.

It is not a foregone conclusion that American cooperation with Nasser would weaken the positions of the kings whom the United States regards as its friends, nor would the security of Lebanese Christians, a strongly anti-Nasser minority, necessarily be threatened. Even assuming that the positions of these Arab elements might be so weakened, the risk must be measured against the overriding American need to stop the Communist advance in the Middle East.

To observers on the scene one thing seems clear: for the United States government to expect President Nasser to abandon "positive neutrality" is at the least futile, since an analysis of the man's character and career indicates he cannot and will not change his stubborn conviction that the Arabs must disentangle themselves from foreign involvement.

It is in just this area of principle that Mr. Nasser's suspicions of the Communists have been aroused. Having become convinced that the Soviet Union aims at controlling Arab affairs, President Nasser is no more likely to forgive Moscow and trust it than he has forgiven and trusts London and Paris—and to some extent Washington—for their past policies in the Arab world. In this sense President Nasser's "positive neutrality" almost certainly cuts both ways.

This does not contradict his evident desire to continue receiving Soviet aid, on which his army and the Egyptian and Syrian economies have grown to depend. To the West it may seem naïve of President Nasser to believe Soviet aid can be accepted harmlessly. But from his point of view Soviet aid falls into the same general class as help from the "imperialist" West, provided both forms of aid are without political conditions. Also the Communist East offers the only sizable market presently open to Egyptian cotton. It need not be assumed that President Nasser is deserting his anti-Communist convictions because he continues to welcome Soviet aid, any more than he has abandoned his anti-imperialist convictions because he now welcomes American technical and economic help.

So far unanswered in all this is whether American support of President Nasser truly will help defeat communism in the Middle East. To the author, and to most experienced observers of his acquaintance, the answer is yes. President Nasser looms as a rallying point for anti-Communist Arabs. Nasser's prestige was considerably dimmed by the failure of the Mosul revolt in Iraq, with which his name had been widely linked, and by the comparative failure of his efforts to subvert the regimes of Saudi Arabia, Jordan, the Sudan, Tunisia, and Lebanon. The distrust with which the leaders of some of these countries continue to regard Mr. Nasser often leads to the obstruction of Egyptian policy in inter-Arab affairs.

But prestige in the Arab world is mercurial, and President Nasser's corraling of Soviet aid to build the High Aswan Dam, his securing of a World Bank loan to improve the Suez Canal, his obvious success at attracting American aid, and his refusal to allow Israeli cargoes through the Suez Canal, all these have repaired some of the damage to his reputation. Through it all President Nasser has continued to wield enormous influence with the common man in the Middle East, and today this influence is directed toward weakening the Communists in the Arab world, including Iraq.

''Communism is not strong numerically in Iraq's Arab neighbors, any more than the Communists were numerous in Iraq before the July, 1958, revolution. But in Syria and Jordan, in particular, economic problems and political unrest provide Communists with the same kind of fertile ground which they exploited in Iraq. To many observers, President Nasser, however unreliable an ally he may prove in the traditional sense, appears the most stable figure around which anti-Communist Arabs can cluster.

The spectacle of American-United Arab Republic cooperation indicates to countless Arabs that the United States has accepted President Nasser on his own terms as leader of the Arab nationalist movement. Such an American policy involves calculated, though possibly only assumed, risks to Israel, to Britain, and to the pro-Western Arab kings. But there is no clear indication that the risks to these powers would be any less if Washington kept Mr. Nasser at pole's length. And to most American observers, it seems evident that the decline of President Nasser at this time would greatly advance Communist interests in the Middle East. ||

President Nasser remains the most popular and influential figure in the Arab world. To oppose or merely to be passive toward the man whom a majority of Arabs regard as their outstanding leader, would only obstruct United States endeavors in the Middle East. It would seem illogical to strive toward area-wide objectives while alienating the vast majority of people who live in the area.

At times American patience and tolerance may be strained by the seemingly incomprehensible things which President Nasser or other Egyptians may do or say. In March, 1960, for example, at a time of Arab-Israel border tension, Israeli Premier David Ben-Gurion went to the United States to receive an honorary degree from Brandeis University. In its issue of March 2, 1960, the U.A.R. Government-owned *Al-Gomhouriya*, edited by Salah Salem, warned the United States against receiving Mr. Ben-Gurion officially.

"We cannot understand America's attitude," *Al-Gomhouriya* fumed, "in welcoming Ben-Gurion who goes there with blood-stained hands from Arab victims and resolutions in the United Nations killed by Israel."[4]  This visit, the newspaper said, showed that the United States ignored Arab rights. If President Eisenhower received Mr. Ben-Gurion, "the filthiest terrorist in existence, it was important for America to guarantee that the doors of Arab friendship would remain open after the visit."[5]

Two days later President Nasser himself spoke in the same vein in a speech delivered in Damascus. Referring to the Brandeis degree for Mr. Ben-Gurion, Nasser said:

How can the biggest war criminal be given such a degree . . . How could a man who killed thousands of innocent men, women, and children be given such a degree? They said Hitler was a war criminal, but did Hitler destroy an entire people as had Ben-Gurion?

Let the United States know that we have taken it upon ourselves to sacrifice our souls and blood. We shall not be under the

[4] *Al-Gomhouriya*, Cairo, March 2, 1960.
[5] *Ibid.*

domination of the United States or Israel. Let them give the war criminal a degree in law. This would make us know the value of law in the United States and the value of man in the United States. It will make us depend on God and ourselves to fight all the battles which may confront us so as to preserve the independence and freedom we won by our souls and our blood.[6]

Most Americans would consider such a statement by a chief of state dangerously irrational. An emotional tirade of this type shows Mr. Nasser at his worst as a demagogic politician. Without doubt many such repetitions by the U.A.R. President would jeopardize the growing cooperation between his government and Washington.

But one phrase in the midst of this diatribe is important to note: "we shall not be under the domination of the United States." At the time that speech was delivered, Arab Communists were working to convince Syrians that Nasser had fallen under the spell of a new imperialism, that of the United States.

Traditionally Syria has been the most anti-Western of all major Arab lands. It was President Nasser who, only shortly before the speech quoted above, had pried open the door of Syria to American technical and economic help. In speaking to his Syrian constituents, the President perhaps felt it imperative to stress anti-Western belligerence. While to Americans this may seem little excuse for the language Nasser used, at least it possibly explains the President's mood. The speech was followed by no move to reduce the network of relations at that time binding Cairo and Washington more closely together. On the contrary, within the month Washington and Cairo signed three agreements involving nearly $47,000,000 worth of new American aid to the U.A.R.

[6] Arab News Agency, Beirut, March 5, 1960.

Worth noting in this respect is a statement which Nasser made to Miles Copeland, an American petroleum economist who is perhaps the one non-Egyptian whom President Nasser regards as a close personal friend. Discussing American policy in the Middle East during the time of Mr. Dulles, Nasser said:

> If you want the cooperation of any Middle Eastern leader, you must first understand his limitations—those limitations placed on him by the emotions and suspicions of the people he leads—and be reconciled to the fact that you can never ask him to go beyond those limitations. If you feel you *must* have him go beyond them, you must be prepared to help him lessen the limitations.

Mr. Nasser went on to say that had he done any one of several things the United States government had asked him to do, he would have been assassinated or overthrown. "And," the Egyptian leader told Mr. Copeland, "if the Secretary of State would make the slightest effort to understand my position, he would see that he is virtually asking me to commit suicide."

It was this line of reasoning which American Embassy officials in Cairo used to dissuade Assistant Secretary of State George Allen from delivering an "ultimatum" to Nasser at the time of the latter's arms deal with Russia.

Recently I spoke with an American diplomat of wide experience in the Middle East. He gave his opinion that, during Mr. Dulles' era, the State Department failed almost entirely to appreciate what Nasser was up against in trying to retain his leadership of an emotional and ignorant people. For example, the diplomat asserted, there were times when those Americans who really comprehended Nasser's situation—whether they liked it or not was beside the point—agreed that Mr. Nasser probably had to take anti-American positions and make anti-American statements. Such a case was Nasser's adverse reaction to the Baghdad Pact, which most Arabs interpreted at the time as a Western device to make the Arabs forget Palestine by conjuring up a Communist enemy.

Yet, the diplomat told me, almost always the State Department resented these statements by Nasser and took them as evidence that the Egyptian was an unreasonable scoundrel. Those officials who tried to convey to Washington an understanding of Nasser's position—Ambassador Byroade was one of them—were labeled "pro-Nasser," and discredited in the eyes of senior officials in Washington. Seeing this, diplomats down the line were quick to realize it was dangerous to follow Mr. Byroade's example. The desire to escape the charge of being "pro-Nasser" became so general, according to the diplomat, that frequently he heard State Department conversations begin with the phrase: "Mind you, I dislike Nasser as much as anybody else . . ."

Each American has the right to decide for himself what elements should go into his government's Middle Eastern policy. A suggested prerequisite of this decision is to start from the standpoint of United States' national interests. When this is done, the necessity is seen for several steps— U.S. alliances with Turkey and Iran, an American guarantee of the integrity of Israel, a similar United States guarantee of Arab frontiers, and cooperative arrangements with individual Arab states.

Of all these strands of policy, only United States relations with Cairo currently are in question, as reflected in Congressional attempts to restrict American aid to the U.A.R. Essentially this means taking sides in the Arab-Israeli dispute. Such favoritism is ill-suited to gaining the trust of the Arabs, among whom the United States has wide and important interests. To serve those interests America must reserve the right to be friends with both sides, now and in the future, when other kings, presidents, and prime ministers may sit in the seats of power.

# Selected Bibliography

ALLEN, ROBERT LORING. *Middle Eastern Economic Relations with the Soviet Union, Eastern Europe, and Mainland China.* Charlottesville: Univ. of Va. Press, 1958.

ANTONIUS, GEORGE. *Arab Awakening: The Story of the Arab National Movement.* Philadelphia: J. B. Lippincott Co., 1939.

CARACTACUS. *Revolution in Iraq.* London: Victor Gollancz, Ltd., 1959.

EDDY, WILLIAM A. *F.D.R. Meets Ibn Saud.* New York: American Friends of the Middle East, Inc., 1954.

ELLIS, HARRY B. *Heritage of the Desert.* New York: The Ronald Press Co., 1956.

———. *Israel and the Middle East.* New York: The Ronald Press Co., 1957.

EYTAN, WALTER. *The First Ten Years.* New York: Simon & Schuster, 1958.

FAIRBANK, JOHN KING. *The United States and China.* Cambridge: Harvard Univ. Press, 1958.

FISHER, SYDNEY NETTLETON. *Social Forces in the Middle East.* Ithaca, N.Y.: Cornell Univ. Press, 1955.

HITTI, PHILIP K. *History of the Arabs,* 6th ed. New York: The Macmillan Co., 1956.

HOFFMAN, PAUL G. *One Hundred Countries—One and One Quarter Billion People.* Washington, D.C.: Albert D. and Mary Lasker Foundation, 1960.

Hoskin, Halford L. *The Middle East: Problem Area in World Politics*. New York: The Macmillan Co., 1954.

Karpat, Kemal H. *Turkey's Politics: The Transition to a Multi-Party System*. Princeton: Princeton Univ. Press, 1959.

Lacouture, Jean and Simonne. *Egypt in Transition*. New York: Criterion Books, Inc., 1958.

Laqueur, Walter Z. *Communism and Nationalism in the Middle East*. New York: Frederick A. Praeger, Inc., 1956.

———. *The Soviet Union and the Middle East*. New York: Frederick A. Praeger, Inc., 1959.

Lenczowski, George. *The Middle East in World Affairs*, 2d ed. Ithaca, N.Y.: Cornell Univ. Press, 1956.

———. *Oil and State in the Middle East*. Ithaca, N.Y.: Cornell Univ. Press, 1960.

Lilienthal, Alfred M. *What Price Israel*. Chicago: Henry Regnery Co., 1953.

Little, Tom. *Egypt*. London: Ernest Benn, Ltd., 1958.

Longrigg, Stephen and Stoakes, Frank. *Iraq*. London: Ernest Benn, Ltd., 1958.

Nasser, Gamal Abdel. *Egypt's Liberation: Philosophy of the Revolution*. Washington, D.C.: Public Affairs Press, 1955.

Overstreet, Harry and Bonaro. *What We Must Know About Communism*. New York: W. W. Norton and Company, Inc., 1958.

Peretz, Don. *Israel and the Palestine Arabs*. Washington, D.C.: The Middle East Institute, 1958.

Royal Institute of International Affairs. *British Interests in the Mediterranean and Middle East*. London: Oxford Univ. Press, 1958.

Smith, Wilfred Cantwell. *Islam in Modern History*. Princeton: Princeton Univ. Press, 1957.

Spector, Ivar. *The Soviet Union and the Muslim World*. Seattle: Univ. of Wash. Press, 1959.

Speiser, E. A. *The United States and the Near East*. Cambridge: Harvard Univ. Press, 1950.

Thomas, Lewis V. and Frye, Richard N. *The United States and Turkey and Iran*. Cambridge: Harvard Univ. Press, 1952.

WALKER, RICHARD L. *China Under Communism*. London: George Allen & Unwin, 1956.

WYNN, WILTON. *Nasser of Egypt*. Cambridge, Mass.: Arlington Books, Inc., 1959.

Periodicals:

The author is grateful for statistical material on Sino-Soviet bloc aid to the Middle East, as well as on United States programs in the area, supplied by the Department of State. Also helpful was a study prepared by Dr. Halford L. Hoskins for Senator Hubert H. Humphrey, entitled "Soviet Economic Penetration in the Middle East." *The Middle East Journal, The New York Times,* and *The Christian Science Monitor* were among American publications used.

# Index

Abboud, Ibrahim, 208, 209
Abdullah, King, 62
Acapulco beach, Lebanon, 9
Afghanistan, 24, 76
   Soviet aid to, 159, 160, 176–78
   U. S. aid to, 177–78
AFL-CIO, 111, 112
Africa, 123–24
Afro-Asian People's Solidarity
   Council, 27
Agricultural Trade and Develop-
   ment and Assistance Act (Pub-
   lic Law 480), 57, 60, 96, 97, 106,
   111, 171, 187, 189
Agriculture, U. S. Department of,
   106
*Al-Ahram* (Cairo newspaper), 15,
   18, 19, 20, 215
*Al-Akhbar* (Cairo newspaper), 13
Aleppo, Syria, 174
Algeria, 27–28, 123
*Al-Gomhouriya* (Cairo news-
   paper), 22, 222
Allen, George V., 44–46, 224
Allen, Robert Loring, 161n
American Jewish Congress, 106
American University of Beirut, 135
American Zionist Organization, 88

Amin, Mustafa, 13–14
Anti-Westernism, 129, 217, 223
Aqaba, Gulf of, 114
Arab League, 104, 115, 131, 208
Arab Legion, 63, 132
Arabian American Oil Company
   (Aramco), 65, 66, 130
Arabs
   anti-Americanism among, 111
   anti-Communist literature and
     the, 13, 14
   anti-Westernism among, 129
   attitude toward Saudi royal fam-
     ily, 66
   attitude toward U. S., 31, 111
   Baghdad Pact and the, 132, 225
   charges of U. S. favoritism to-
     ward, 107
   "Cleopatra" incident and the, 113
   Communism and, 22, 26, 29, 221
   education of, 135
   Israel and the, 62, 78, 100, 114–20
   Jordan River project and the,
     102, 104
   Lebanese crisis and the, 73
   Palestine dispute and the, 87, 91–
     92, 94

Arabs—*Continued*
  Russia and the, 42
  settlements in Lebanon, 7–8
  U. S. aid to, 96, 97
  U. S. government blackmailed
    by, 106
  U. S. relations with, 114–20, 131,
    132, 135–36, 212, 221, 225–26
  unity among, 51, 63, 113
Asha, Hafik, 113
Associated Press, 44, 45, 121n, 216
"Astypalea" (Greek ship), 102
Aswan Dam project, 26, 47, 48, 59,
    100, 162–64, 170, 181, 182, 220
Attlee, Clement, 88, 89

Baghdad, Iraq, 23, 24, 86, 143–45
Baghdad Pact, 14, 38, 40, 74, 131–33,
    160, 225
Bahrein Petroleum Company, 125
Basra, Iraq, 26
Bayar, Celal, 80, 81, 82
Beirut, Lebanon, 7, 8, 117, 151, 202–
    4
Ben-Gurion, David, 88, 98, 222
Beria, Lavrenti, 18
Bibliography, 227–29
Biltmore Program, 88
Birth control, 182
Bitar, Salah, 52
Bitter Lakes, 56
Bombay Port Trust General Work-
    ers Union, 112
Bourguiba, President, 207–8
Brandeis University, 222
Bulganin, Nikolai, 18
Bulgaria, 174
Burma, 118
Byroade, Henry A., 37–39, 42, 44,
    45, 46, 55, 225

Caffrey, Jefferson, 36, 37, 38
Cairo, Egypt, 12–20, 22, 23, 24, 26,
    27, 28, 31, 41, 55, 57
Canada, 15, 16, 167, 168, 188
CARE, 46, 56

Carlan, Thomas J., 191
Carroll, Wallace E., 191
Case, Clifford P., 105
Central Treaty Organization
    (CENTO), 74, 75, 79, 123, 132
Chamoun, Camille, 40, 68–70, 72,
    73, 134, 205
Chehab, Fuad, 72, 73, 204, 205, 209
China
  Communist, 161, 164, 172, 176
  Nationalist, 90, 91
Chinese-Egyptian Friendship So-
    ciety, 25
Chinese-Iraqi Friendship Society,
    24
Chirurg, James Thomas, 191
"Cleopatra" (U.A.R. ship), 109–
    13
Commerce, U. S. Department of,
    190, 191, 200
Commodity Credit Corporation,
    106
Communism, 12–28, 35, 53, 122–24,
    133, 143–79, 180, 220, 221
Constantinople Convention (1888),
    101
Copeland, Miles, 224
Cotton, Egyptian, 29, 47, 161, 165,
    166–67, 169, 172, 175, 180, 181,
    191, 192
Cyprus, 50
Czechoslovakia, 29, 161, 164, 165,
    172, 174

Damascus, Syria, 26, 28, 32, 33, 61,
    118, 174
Defense Department, U. S., 106
Denmark, 174
Development Loan Fund, 60, 96,
    186, 187, 189, 196
Dewey, Thomas E., 89
Dhahran airfield, 65, 106, 107, 130
Dillon, Douglas, 108, 112, 113
Douglas, Paul H., 108, 110
Dulles, John Foster, 37, 38, 39, 40,
    46, 47, 50, 52, 53, 65, 71, 131,
    133, 134, 163, 224

Eddy, William A., 91
Egypt; *see also* United Arab Republic
  agrarian reform in, 183–85
  Arab-Jewish war and, 92
  attitude toward Communism, 12–30
  Baghdad Pact and, 131
  birth control in, 182
  cotton; *see* Cotton, Egyptian
  economy, 181–86
  Eisenhower Doctrine and, 134
  High Aswan Dam; *see also* Aswan Dam project
  industrialization plan, 181
  invasion by Britain, France, and Israel, 14, 50, 97, 163
  New Valley project, 58–59
  relations with other Arab countries, 205–11
  Soviet aid to, 159–76
  Suez Canal; *see* Suez Canal
  U. S. aid to, 96
  U. S. relations with, 30, 31–86, 98, 189, 204–25
Egyptian-American Rural Improvement Service (EARIS), 57
Eisenhower, Dwight D., 44, 72, 86, 97, 102, 109, 113, 121, 186, 190, 196, 222
Eisenhower Doctrine, 69, 70, 132, 133–34
el-Assali, Sabri, 52
Elath, Israel, 114
Eshkol, Levi, 103
"Essayon" (U. S. Army dredge), 56
Ethiopia, 90, 91
Euphrates River Dam, 174
Export Control Act (1949), 97–98
Export-Import Bank, 58, 96, 187, 196

Farouk, King, 34, 35
Feisal, King, 53, 66, 147, 205, 209, 214

Fulbright, J. William, 108, 109–10, 111

Gaza, 40, 41, 115, 117, 118
Germany
  East, 161, 164, 174
  West, 161, 168, 170, 188
Ghana, 118
Goldberg, Arthur J., 112
Greece, 90, 91, 160
Gursel, Cemal, 80, 81, 82, 85

"Haifa clause," 105
Haiti, 90, 91
Hall, Paul, 109, 111, 113
Hammarskjold, Dag, 100, 101–2
Hare, Raymond A., 38, 51, 55, 71
Hart, Parker K., 121, 122
Hawk, E. Paul, 191, 192
Helmand Valley project, 178
Herter, Christian A., 134
Heykal, Mohammed, 15, 17, 18, 215–16
High Aswan Dam; *see* Aswan Dam project
Hinnawi, Sami, 33
Hitler, Adolf, 222
Holy Land, 88, 89
Homs, Syria, 174
Horowitz, David, 99
Hourani, Akram, 52
Huck, William F., 191
Hungary, 12, 13, 14, 15, 172, 174
Hussein, King, 40, 51, 62–63, 129, 132, 179, 205–7, 212, 213, 214 219

Ilah, Abdul, 147
Independent Producers Association of America, 124
India, 112, 123, 161
"Inge Toft" (Danish freighter), 100, 102
Inonu, Ismet, 81, 82
International Bank for Reconstruction and Development (World Bank), 58, 100, 102, 163, 187–88, 196, 220

International Cooperation Administration, 195
International Development Association (IDA), 188
International Federation of Arab Trade Unions, 110
International Longshoremen's Association, 109
International Monetary Fund, 168, 188
Investment Guaranty Program, 187, 195–97
Iran
 Afghanistan's threat to, 176–78
 Central Treaty Organization and, 132–33
 Communism in, 25–26
 Israeli mission in, 118
 land reform, 137–42
 oil, 125
 Soviet Union and, 160
 U. S. relations with, 74–79, 86, 212, 225
 water supply, 3–6
Iraq
 anti-Communist literature in, 13
 Arab-Jewish war, 92
 Baghdad Pact, 131, 132, 133, 160
 Communism in, 17–26, 179, 180, 181, 221
 Eisenhower Doctrine and, 134
 Nasser and, 208–11
 oil, 125, 185
 poverty in, 185
 revolution (1958), 59–60, 64, 76
 sentiment for union of Syria with, 33
 Soviet and, 76, 143–59, 165, 169, 174, 175, 197
 U. S. aid to, 96, 130
 U. S. policy toward, 64
 U. S. relations with, 86, 98, 189, 197–201, 220
Iraq Development Board, 145–48
Iraq Petroleum Company, 125, 152, 157

Israel
 Arab-Israeli relations, 32, 135
 Egyptian-Israeli relations, 40–45, 62, 64
 establishment of State of, 92, 160
 French aid to, 22
 invasion of Egypt, 14, 50, 97, 163
 Nasser and, 213–14
 relations with Iran, 78–79
 U. N. and, 214–17
 U. S. policy toward, 50–51
 U. S. relations with, 20, 31, 86, 87–120, 131, 212
Italy, 161, 168

Japan, 162, 188, 189
Jerusalem, 90
Jewish Agency, 88
Johnston, Eric, 44, 45, 102
Johnston Plan, 102
Jordan
 Baghdad Pact and, 132
 Communism in, 26, 179, 221
 Palestinian refugees in, 118
 relations with Egypt, 205–7, 208
 relations with U. S., 61–65, 86, 98
 U. S. aid to, 96, 97, 129, 134, 186, 214
Jordan River, 64, 102–4, 179

Kabul River, hydroelectric project on the, 177
Kaganovitch, Lazar, 18
Karami, Rashid, 72–73
Karanjia, R. K., 19
Kassem, Abdel Karim, 17, 18, 22, 23, 64, 86, 132, 143, 147–50, 152–53, 156, 175, 189, 197, 199, 209, 211
Keating, Kenneth B., 108, 110
Kelly, Charles J., 191
Kerbala, Iraq, 26
Khalil, Abdullah, 208
Khedivial Mail Line, 110
Khrushchev, Nikita S., 18–22, 180
Kirkuk uprising, 25
Kubbeh, Ibrahim, 149, 153, 156

Kurds, 21, 33, 76
Kuwait, 19, 127
Kuwait Oil Company, 125
Kuwatly, Shukri, 32–33, 52

Lakeland, William, 35
Land reform, Iranian, 137–42
Lasso, Galo Plaza, 71
Latafiyah, Iraq, 150–51
Lebanon
    Arab-Jewish war, 92
    "Cleopatra" incident and, 110
    Communist bloc trade with, 179
    Jordan River project, 102
    Nasser and, 209, 211, 220
    Palestinian refugees in, 118
    people of, 7–10
    pro-Nasser demonstrations in, 202–5
    U. S. aid to, 96, 134
    U. S. relations with, 67–74, 86, 98
Lehman, Herbert, 89
Lenczowski, George, 125n
Liberia, 90, 91
Libya, 13, 85, 86, 127, 131, 135, 210–11
*Life* (magazine), 12

MacAndrews & Forbes, 157
Mahdawi, Fadhel Abbas, 25
Malenkov, Georgi, 18
Malik, Charles, 69, 70–71
Mansour race track (Iraq), 151–52
McClintock, Robert W., 70, 72
Mead, James M., 89
Meany, George, 111, 112
Menderes, Adnan, 80–85
Middle East Emergency Committee, 126
Mikoyan, Anastas I., 150–51
Mitchell, James, 111, 112
Morocco, 13, 85, 86
Mosul, Iraq, 26
Murphy, Robert, 72
Mutual Security Program, 186–87

Naguib, Mohammed, 36, 38
Najaf, Iraq, 26

Nasser, Gamal Abdel
    agrarian reform under, 83
    anti-Westernism, 38, 213, 217
    appeal for U. S. aid, 41–42
    Aswan Dam project, 163, 170
    attitude toward birth control, 182
    attitude toward Communism, 12–22, 26–30, 124, 176, 180
    attitude toward U. S., 36–37, 39, 51, 54
    Baghdad Pact and, 40
    "Cleopatra" incident, 111
    Dulles and, 39, 40, 46, 50
    Egypt's development plans under, 59, 169, 181
    Israel and, 213–17
    Jordan and, 64
    Lebanese crisis and, 71, 73
    Lebanon and, 68–69
    merger of Egypt and Syria, 52
    Palestine problem and, 40, 41
    popularity in other Arab-countries, 204–12
    problems faced by, 130
    refusal to allow Israeli cargoes through Suez Canal, 100–102, 216–17, 221
    relations with Ambassador Byroade, 37–38, 39
    rise of, 35, 38
    Saudi Arabia and, 66
    Soviet aid offered to, 42–46
    Suez Canal nationalized by, 48
    U. S. attitude toward, 31, 34–35, 49, 53, 86
    U. S. relations with, 213–26
"National Peace" (tanker), 104
National Shipping and Trading Corporation, 104–5
Negev, 102, 103, 104
New China News Agency (Hsin-hua), 24
New Valley project (Egypt), 58–59
North Atlantic Treaty Organization, 79, 123

Nuri es-Said, Premier, 40, 64, 132, 134, 143, 146, 147, 159
Nuwar, Ali Abu, 63

Oil, 124–28, 159, 171, 181, 185
Omran (Development) Bank, 139–40
Organization for European Economic Cooperation, 84

Pakistan, 106, 107, 123, 132, 133, 134, 177, 178
Palestine, 31, 33, 34, 40, 62, 87–95, 114–18, 131, 135, 214–15, 225
Palestine Arab Congress, 115
Pan Cargo Shipping Corporation, 104–5
Pasha, Glubb, 132
Philippines, 90, 91
Point Four Program, 57, 60, 130, 175, 186, 187, 189, 195
Port Said, Egypt, 56, 101, 102
Public Law 480; see Agricultural Trade and Development and Assistance Act
"Pushtoonistan," 177

Qatar, 125
Qum, Iran, 3–5

Ram, Houshang, 139, 141–42
Ras Tanura, Saudi Arabia, 104
Red Crescent Society, 144
Reza Pahlevi, Shah Mohammed, 74, 76–78, 137–42
Roosevelt, Franklin D., 88
Roosevelt, Kermit, 35, 36, 43, 45, 89 n.
Rountree, William M., 121–22
Russia; see Soviet Union

Sahl Batouf reservoir, 103
Salem, Salah, 22, 222
Salter, Lord, 146
Sami es-Solh, Prime Minister, 70
Saud, King, 53, 65–67, 214, 219

Saudi Arabia, 53, 62, 65–66, 91, 96, 104, 106, 107, 125, 129, 131, 134–35, 179, 205, 209, 211, 212, 214, 220
   U. S. relations with, 65–67, 86, 98
Sayegh, Dr. Fayez, 115
Seafarers International Union, 109, 111, 112, 113
Serraj, Abdel Hamid, 53, 60
Shahidi, Burhan, 24–25
Shepilov, Dimitri, 48
Shishakly, Adib, 33
Sidon, Lebanon, 204
Sinai, Israeli conquest of, 92, 98
Southeast Asia Treaty Organization (SEATO), 123
Soviet Union
   Aswan Dam project and, 100
   Nasser's attitude toward, 219–20
   oil and, 127
   penetration in the Middle East, 143–79, 180
   possibility of attack on Iran, 75–76
   relations with Egypt, 15–30, 42–44, 46, 47, 48, 53, 133
   Soviet build-up in Iraq and Afghanistan, 76
   Turkey and, 79
Stalin, Joseph, 18, 160
State Department, U. S., 31, 34, 42, 45, 46, 47, 49, 51, 55, 58, 71, 89, 98, 106, 107, 108, 112, 113, 190, 218, 224, 225
"Struggle of Hungary for Freedom, The" (booklet), 14
Sudan, 13, 47, 85, 86, 96, 98, 130, 161, 167, 179, 183, 208, 209, 220
Suez Canal, 56, 58, 100–102, 104, 108–10, 113–14, 125, 169, 175, 215, 220, 221
   barred to Israeli shipping, 100
   nationalization of the, 48–49, 163
Suez Canal Company, 48–49, 163
Suez Canal Users' Association, 49–50

Suez Canal Zone, 36
Suleimaniyah, Iraq, 26
Syria; *see also* United Arab Republic
  American intervention in, 31–34, 51
  anti-Westernism in, 223
  Arab-Jewish war, 92
  Communism in, 221
  *coup d'etat* in, 33
  economy of, 185
  Eisenhower Doctrine and, 134
  Jordan River project, 102, 103
  land reform in, 6
  Lebanese crisis and, 69, 71
  merger with Egypt, 26, 52–53
  Nasser and, 209–10
  Palestinian refugees in, 116, 117, 118
  Soviet aid to, 20, 159–76
  U. S. aid to, 60–61, 111, 189

Tartous, Syria, 173
Tass, 24
Technical Cooperation program; *see* Point Four Program
Tourism, 193–95
Trade missions, 191–96
Trading with the Enemy Act (1941), 97
Tripoli, Lebanon, 204
Truman, Harry S., 79, 88, 89, 91, 93, 160
Tunisia, 85, 86, 207–8, 220
Turkey, 26, 132, 133, 134, 160, 178
  U. S. relations with, 79–85, 86, 212, 225

Union of South Africa, 123
Union of Soviet Socialist Republics; *see* Soviet Union
United Arab Republic; *see also* Egypt; Syria
  anti-Communist literature in, 13–14
  Aswan Dam; *see* Aswan Dam project
  "Cleopatra" incident, 109–13
  establishment of, 52–53
  Gaza and the, 118
  Lebanon and the, 68–69, 71, 73
  Soviet aid to, 17–20, 133, 162–64
  Soviet relations with, 17–29, 162–66, 169–76, 180
  students, overseas, 15–16
  Suez Canal; *see* Suez Canal
  U. S. aid to, 56–57, 59–61, 97, 98, 100, 111, 134, 181, 186, 189, 201, 223
  U. S. relations with, 55–57, 59, 86, 119, 130, 167, 212, 221
  U. S. trade mission to, 191–96
United Jewish Appeal, 95
United Nations, 100, 103, 104, 113, 122, 160, 187, 188, 214, 215, 216
  Emergency Force, 114
  Expanded Program of Technical Assistance, 59
  Lebanese question, 70–71
  Palestine dispute, 90–92, 214–17
United Nations Relief and Works Agency (UNRWA), 115, 116, 117, 118
United States
  Afghanistan and, 177–78
  Baghdad Pact and, 132
  Egypt and, 30, 31–86, 98, 204–25
  interests in the Middle East, 121–42
  Iran and, 74–79, 86
  Iraq and, 86, 98
  Israel and, 86, 87–120
  Jordan and, 61–65, 86, 98
  Lebanon and, 67–74, 86, 98
  Saudi Arabia and, 65–67, 86, 98
  Turkey and, 79–85, 86
United States Geologic Survey, 58
United States Information Service (U.S.I.S.), 14, 86
U.S.S.R.; *see* Soviet Union

Wadsworth, George, 31, 91, 92
Water supply, in Iran, 3–6

"What Happens When Communism Enters a Country" (booklet), 12–14
Wheelus Field, 86
White, Lincoln, 107
World Bank; *see* International Bank for Reconstruction and Development
World Zionist Organization, 88
Wynn, Wilton, 49n, 216

Yemen, 13
  Soviet aid to, 159, 176
Youssef, Salah Ben, 208
Yugoslavia, 174
Yunes, Mahmoud, 49

Zaim, Husni, 32–33, 34
Zionists, 31, 50, 88–91, 95, 107, 111, 112, 113, 119, 212